CLEVELAND CURIOSITIES

CLEVELAND CURIOSITIES

ELIOT NESS & HIS BLUNDERING RAID

A BUSKER'S PROMISE

THE RICHEST HEIRESS WHO NEVER LIVED

AND

MORE

TED SCHWARZ

Charleston London

THE History PRESS

Published by The History Press
Charleston, SC 29403
www.historypress.net

First published 2010

Manufactured in the United States

ISBN 978.1.59629.919.1

Library of Congress Cataloging-in-Publication Data

Schwarz, Ted, 1945-

Cleveland curiosities : Eliot Ness and his blundering raid, a busker's promise, the richest
heiress who never lived, and more / Ted Schwarz.

p. cm.

ISBN 978-1-59629-919-1

1. Cleveland (Ohio)--Biography--Anecdotes. 2. Celebrities--Ohio--Cleveland--Biography--
Anecdotes. 3. Curiosities and wonders--Ohio--Cleveland--Anecdotes. 4. Cleveland (Ohio)-
-History--Anecdotes. 5. Cleveland (Ohio)--Social life and customs--Anecdotes. I. Title.

F499.C653A28 2010

977.1'32--dc22

2010042768

Contents

Eliot Ness? You Just Thought You Knew Him

You can get more with a kind word and a gun than you can with a kind word alone.
—*Quote from Chicago's notorious bootlegger, brothel operator and all-around bad guy Al Capone*

Gossip is the art of saying nothing in a way that leaves practically nothing unsaid.
—*Walter Winchell*

I usually get my stuff from people who promised somebody else that they would keep it a secret.
—*Walter Winchell*

Gossip columnist Walter Winchell and former Cleveland public safety director Eliot Ness were two men on the downward slope of fame. Walter Winchell was not the first gossip columnist in America, but in the pre–World War II years, he was arguably the hardest working and most influential. He knew everyone and celebrated everyone, so long as their names in print could generate office gossip the day they appeared. Owen "Owney the Killer" Madden, a mob guy and the rare individual who left the rackets alive to retire on a substantial holding of ill-gotten gains, was a friend and subject. Likewise, FBI Director J. Edgar Hoover considered Winchell a friend because the newsman deliberately wrote laudatory column items about him.

Winchell was heard on radio. He was read in newspapers from coast to coast, a fact that inspired other media giants to hire their own personnel. Louella Parsons and Hedda Hopper, Syd Skolsky and Earl Wilson, Ed

Sullivan and Jim Bacon all were getting their turns. As a result, the attention Winchell once commanded was being dissipated in the 1950s. His income was down to where he needed to find someone who would be exclusively his and renew his column's "must-read" cachet. The answer was a dead man.

Two decades earlier, when Eliot Ness was head of the U.S. Treasury Department's alcohol tax unit's "get-Capone squad," he became the best-known lawman in America by being the first to have a comic strip based on fantasies about his exploits. Not that the Ness name was used. Cartoonist Chester Gould, the comic strip artist and writer, called his version of Ness "Dick Tracy," but Ness, Hoover and Winchell knew the truth, and it infuriated Hoover. It also helped refine the myth of Ness's career in Chicago before he came to Cleveland.

Ness, born in Chicago in 1903, graduated from the University of Chicago in 1925, near the end of Prohibition. His classes were mostly business related, and it would be as a businessman at the end of the Prohibition era that Al Capone was eventually jailed.

Capone was a bootlegger who also operated a nationwide delivery service for other bootleggers needing their liquor shipped from where it was either manufactured or smuggled into the United States. He ran gambling operations. He engaged in extortion. And because of youthful indiscretions with willing young women, he had syphilis, which had gone untreated for so many years that it was essentially a death sentence waiting to happen. It also made Capone extremely volatile—the reason so many of his enemies were killed in unusually brutal ways. But despite the image of Ness and the men who worked with him as being incorruptible—"Untouchables," they were called, because they rejected all bribes—the dangers they faced in their pursuit of Capone were limited. Violent shootouts, car chases and the like; a mainstay of books about Capone and Ness; a television show based on Ness's self-serving autobiography; and at least one motion picture did not happen. Al Capone was brought to justice because he was too cheap and too greedy to pay taxes.

Capone, who obviously lived well, could have declared income that matched his lifestyle, paid taxes accordingly and kept the difference between what was reported and what was paid. Instead, he thought he was being smart by keeping it all and paying nothing, never realizing that under the law he was showing himself to be indigent. A man with no visible means of support and claiming none was considered a vagrant and could be jailed as such. This was the justification for the arrest of Capone, giving the federal officers time to build a case for income tax evasion. Capone was convicted and sent to prison, where his health deteriorated due to syphilis. After being paroled from prison, Capone died in seclusion at his home in Palm Beach, Florida, of a stroke followed by pneumonia.

The public eventually came to believe the myth that Capone met Ness, presumably the tougher of the two men, in a violent showdown and that the conviction was based on Capone's violent criminal empire. In truth, Ness and the other federal officers had no blazing firefights with Capone with Thompson submachine guns ("Tommy guns"), no close combat with handguns and no hand-to-hand combat (though Ness was a judo practitioner). And Capone's brothels, bootlegging and gambling joints continued business almost as usual under the direction of hand-picked Capone subordinates.

(About fifteen years following Ness's death, the last survivor of the Untouchable agents was teaching police academy classes as part of his job with the division of Alcohol, Tobacco and Firearms. He told the officers about the work they did with Ness in Chicago and Cleveland, laughing about the fact that when five o'clock came around, they often went drinking. They knew where to get the best Prohibition-era liquor.)

Ness might never have come to the attention of Cleveland's civic leaders if it hadn't been for what could be called the cult of Al Capone. Writers from around the world were fascinated with the idea of American gangsters in general and Capone in particular. He was an expert at creating short, amusing quips that were quoted by columnists and repeated by office workers and others. He also had a number of biographers, most of whom had never met him, had never met anyone who knew him and, in some cases, had never been to the United States.

Typical was author Jack Bilbo's "autobiography," *Carrying a Gun for Al Capone: The Intimate Experiences of a Gangster in the Bodyguard of Al Capone*. The book, it was discovered later, was written by British author Hugo C.K. Baruch. The man called Jack Bilbo did not exist, and Baruch may have done little more than read a few newspaper or magazine stories about Capone, Chicago and the era as it was being experienced in the United States before letting his imagination run free.

The public never cared. A good story, well written, could always trump the truth. As a result, Baruch's book became a bestseller and stayed in print for sixteen years. It was also used as one of the "factual" accounts that served as a resource for other biographers of Capone.

ELIOT NESS IS DICK TRACY

This American system of ours, call it Americanism, call it capitalism, call it what you will, gives each and every one of us a great opportunity if we only seize it with both hands and make the most of it.
—*Al Capone*

I have built my organization upon fear.
—*Al Capone*

In a curiosity of those days, the three men who had the greatest skill in manipulating the media to look upon them as either heroes or counterculture characters were FBI Director J. Edgar Hoover, Al Capone and Eliot Ness, whose ultimate goal was to join the FBI. He made himself available to the media and made certain that his actions in Chicago were reported favorably. As head of the Capone squad, his name was regularly in the newspapers, regardless of his importance relative to one case or another. He would simply become better known.

What Ness failed to realize was that, by the time he came to Cleveland, his arrogance and fame angered Hoover, who vowed he would never hire Ness. But as much as Hoover wanted to downplay the importance of Ness in the fight against crime, others used his image to create a popular culture hero.

In 1931, Ness achieved the pop culture reputation that would propel him to Cleveland. Cartoonist Chester Gould was trying to find characters and a story line that would hold the interest of the American public. Prohibition had given enormous power to the mob. Some mobsters had gained the same status as other successful owners of high-profit businesses. People enjoyed bootleg booze, gambling and more traditional entertainment such as bands and attractive singers in a variety of both large and small locations. The customers liked knowing the men who ran them, knowing that when they entered one of the illegal establishments they would be greeted by name, believing that the gangsters saw them as equals when it came to respect.

But the fantasy ended when children coming home from school spotted an occasional bullet-riddled body or elderly women leaving church encountered the aftermath of a bombing. Men who failed to meet their gambling operations were badly beaten, and the families of consistent losers, men who "welshed" on their bets, were threatened with violence.

The mob might brag that it only killed its own, but death was often meant to send a message and thus had to be publicly known. A corpse needed to be left in plain sight; a bombing or arson needed to take place where there would be witnesses. Whatever the reasoning, civilians might not be hurt, but they would be exposed to horrors they did not want to see. And because the bad guys acted with seeming impunity, the public became increasingly outraged over a Cleveland legal system in which arrests were few and convictions fewer.

In one outrageous incident, for example, two Cleveland brothers, owners of a Mayfield Road restaurant, shot a man for whatever failure earned the mob's death penalty. The man managed to crawl out of the restaurant, sprawling on the sidewalk and dying just outside the front door.

The homicide detectives who were called to the murder scene immediately went inside the restaurant, outraged over the murder. As the story would later be told, the detectives reminded the brothers that they were supposed to keep their murders *inside* their restaurant. The moment a victim made his way outside, the public demanded that they investigate the crime. Worse, if there were witnesses to the shooting who were willing to talk, the detectives would have to arrest the killer. This was presumably a moral outrage typical of the warped sense of justice and decency that defined the era. "Next time," the detectives allegedly told the brothers, "kill the guy in your restaurant. Then we don't have to do anything." (The brother who was the triggerman had to flee to Mexico to avoid jail. He then moved back up into the Southwestern states, eventually becoming involved in the creation of Las Vegas. He apparently never returned to Cleveland, though family members continued to live in the city.)

The Cleveland citizenry, as well as many in Chicago, New York, Providence, Boston and other cities where corruption ruled, hated the influence of the criminals yet knew that complaints would likely lead to a beating or worse. What they wanted was a vigilante, a man who would do whatever was necessary to achieve justice and peace, even if it meant shooting any bad guy who might be freed by a court of law. And while no living person fit the image of the desired hero, Chester Gould created the hero everyone desired—Dick Tracy.

Gould later admitted that he modeled Dick Tracy on what he had heard and read about Eliot Ness and his battle with Capone.

It is uncertain what aspects of Ness inspired Chester Gould, but Dick Tracy was afraid of no one, used his gun to shoot bad guys, who otherwise might have gone free, and could not be bribed. He was also high tech. At a time when patrol cars could only receive messages and officers needing to respond to the dispatcher would have to stop at a specially marked telephone call box meant only for law enforcement use, Dick Tracy's men had two-way wrist radios. This was years before the invention of the transistor made even thinking about the electronic engineering of such devices possible.

Gould went further. The Sunday *Dick Tracy* comic strip ended with a panel providing information meant to fight crime and keep the public safe. The ideas were under a heading called "Crime Stoppers Textbook." And it was all based on a man who had gained great publicity for himself but who had never met Gould or the other writers. However, by the time Walter Winchell needed to supplement his income, he decided to hitch his future to a myth he, in part, created and, almost alone, maintained. This myth was Eliot Ness, and by the time he was needed by Winchell, Ness was both disgraced and dead.

THE MAN BEHIND THE MYTH

Nothing recedes like success.
—*Walter Winchell*

Ness came to Cleveland in August 1934, his reputation for integrity and successful law enforcement in a corrupt city dominated by criminal activity preceding him. His transfer by the U.S. Treasury Department's alcohol tax unit was a promotion to head of the enforcement division, where he was expected to use more of his forensic accounting skills than any skill with a weapon or unarmed combat.

Ness was a man with a goal. He worked hard in Cleveland because he wanted to eventually join the FBI. He had gained favorable, if a bit exaggerated, attention in Chicago, and Cleveland was seemingly as corrupt. There were illegal gambling joints allowed to operate. "Professional women" were available both as outcall and in brothels that were occasionally in the backrooms or upstairs from otherwise legitimate restaurants or similar enterprises. And every major crime figure in the East and Midwest had some sort of connection to groups such as the Mayfield Road Gang; the Jewish Combination (Jewish, Italian and Greek); Detroit's Purple Gang, some of whose members, such as Moe Dalitz, eventually worked out of Cleveland; and others.

As for Ness, he hoped to parlay the work he did and the myth that surrounded his past into a position with the FBI. He did not realize that his shameless self-promotion, so similar to that of the director himself, outraged Hoover, who wanted to maintain sole possession of the biggest ego in Washington.

Not that any of the hostility between Hoover and Ness was known outside of the bureau. It took the deaths of both men and the eventual release of Ness's FBI file to reveal the truth. And while there was much Ness accomplished as a result of his Cleveland work and the job he obtained immediately after, there was a tragic-comic side to the man that has generally been forgotten.

In December 1935, more than sixteen months after he came to Cleveland, reform mayoral candidate Harold Hitz Burton asked Ness to leave the federal government and take the job of Cleveland safety director. The job seemed a way to prove his versatility, and so Ness was delighted to accept the position. He was especially told to target the Mayfield Road Gang and its illegal gambling operations, something Ness approached with enthusiasm, limited skill and ultimate failure. He was able to improve law enforcement training for the police officers, rid the department of the entrenched corruption among older officers and modernize their equipment. But he failed miserably at such routine police work as the pursuit of a serial killer who came to be known as "the butcher of Kingsbury Run," and he never did stop the Mayfield Road gang as Burton thought he would do.

Before Ness acquired enough of a record for the Cleveland public to reflect on his failing to meet some of the challenges for which he was supposedly so well equipped, there were many moneyed residents who thought he might make an excellent mayor. Such a success would have allowed him to transition into a retirement during which he would tell war stories to anyone buying him a drink.

It was his alcoholic gregariousness that would cause him problems. By 1942, excessive booze, excessive women (Emma, Evaline and, soon, Elizabeth, as well as girlfriends and casual partners) and the no-longer-fawning newspaper stories led him to seek a new enemy to conquer. Oddly, this was not a gangster, a killer or a bank robber. Instead, it was the sexually transmitted disease known as syphilis, the same condition that deteriorated Al Capone's health and led to his death after his release on parole.

It is impossible to know why syphilis became Ness's obsession or indirectly the cause of his resigning from the Cleveland public safety director position. What is known is that while working in Cleveland, he wrote an article on syphilis that appeared in the March 1942 issue of the *Annals of the American Academy of Political and Social Sciences*. It was not something about which he could brag within his Cleveland social circle, but he and Evaline thought it was worth celebrating on the night of March 4 by drinking steadily with their friends until 4:30 a.m.

Too drunk to drive but not sober enough to realize that fact, the couple drove on what was then the Bulkley Boulevard, the fastest route through the west side of Cleveland, into the adjoining community of Lakewood, where they lived. The road was icy, the night was dark and Ness went too fast with too little control. His car went into a long skid, veering into the oncoming lane and smashing into a car driven by twenty-one-year-old Robert Sims.

Sims did not recognize the drunk who struck him when the driver staggered over to his car to see if he was alive. However, Sims did make a note of the license plate of the other car—EN-3.

The drunk left the scene, but other drivers happened by and arranged to get Sims to a hospital for treatment. Later, Ness admitted that he drove home in his partially wrecked but still serviceable car.

Perhaps there had been a time in his Cleveland career when the police would have left the safety director alone. However, between the vanity plate and the hypocrisy Ness had shown too frequently of late, the police were outraged. They tracked him down and charge him with being a hit-and-run driver.

Ness, recognizing that he could not run, faced the press and announced that though he had been drinking, he was not drunk: "It was very slippery, and the thing happened just like that." He also diminished his responsibility to Sims. He said that he had been about to follow Sims to the hospital when his wife said she was hurting from striking the dashboard. Instead of evading responsibility, he claimed to have met the greater need of his wife by taking her home.

Clevelanders were incensed. The womanizing drunk had lied to the city he should have been serving, and he was forced to resign on April 30, 1942. Soon, the man who claimed to be the scourge of Al Capone and all the bad guys in Cleveland would use the notoriety from the publication he and his wife had been celebrating the night of the Sims crash to take on his number one nemesis: sex with the wrong kind of woman.

DON'T KISS HER, SOLDIER. SHE'S THE *REAL* ENEMY IN THIS WAR

It was the dirty little secret of World War II, an enemy Eliot Ness called "Military Saboteur Number One," expecting the public to see his latest battle in the same light as when he allegedly faced down the deadliest of gangsters: Public Enemy Number One.

Eliot Ness? You Just Thought You Knew Him

Who were these people, this evil force that threatened America's best-trained, bravest and toughest young men? Who could be of such importance that a man who was still seen as a national hero, albeit no longer by Clevelanders, would dedicate his days and nights to the enemy's defeat? The answer was simple—women (though presumably not the ones whose physical company *he* enjoyed).

Yes, women, or more precisely, sexually willing women.

(This was an era when football coaches warned the players on their teams against making love the night before a game because sex robbed a man of his essential essence. And when it came to going into battle, a soldier probably would not have the opportunity to endanger his "essence," but he could carry a dangerous, unwanted souvenir back to his unit—syphilis.)

Ness, temporarily fleeing Cleveland, parlayed his academic article into a Washington, D.C. job as director of the Social Protection Division, Office of Community War Services, Federal Security Agency. It was a great title, important sounding, and he hoped it might be impressive enough to get him a job with the FBI.

Not that Ness had been offered such a position. J. Edgar Hoover hated the publicity-seeking, often incompetent Ness, who managed to frequently get more attention than the…publicity-seeking, often incompetent FBI director. One oversized ego was enough in a major Washington, D.C.–headquartered law enforcement agency. That was why Ness's loss in Cleveland was the nation's gain in the form of a pamphlet entitled *What About Girls?*

The pamphlet combines medical information, cautionary tales and a bit of prudishness from a man with a reputation for being a womanizer. The following is excerpted from the section "How They May Be Caught":

> Both syphilis and gonorrhea are caught through intimate contact with an infected person. *I say "intimate contact" instead of sexual intercourse because I don't want you to think you're safe if you use a rubber or don't go all the way. Necking a girl who has syphilis or gonorrhea gives the germs plenty of chances to make contact with you.*
>
> *It is* possible *to get either of these diseases by using an article freshly soiled by an infected person. But my medical friends tell me that those rare cases are very difficult to prove. The germs scarcely live long enough to attack an innocent bystander. So when a fellow who has caught a disease suddenly remembers using somebody's towel, washrag, or toothbrush by mistake—then's the time to "cherchez la femme." And I mean it.* Look for the woman *so that she can be given treatment, too.*

The cautionary tales within the pamphlet are all meant to scare soldiers from seeking sex with any female—fiancées, patriotic girls (often the "girl next door" type of innocent who wants to give a soldier a happy memory when he goes overseas to fight the enemy) and prostitutes alike. And among these is the story of "The Pick-up Bride," one that would read like a quirky message from an overly exuberant evangelist for abstinence if it hadn't been written by the formerly famous Eliot Ness:

> *I'd like to tell you, too, about the one man in ten who was infected by his wife. That marriage was as casual as a pick-up. They had never met before his buddy introduced them in a juke joint near Camp B. They had no common roots. The girl had wandered from one camp-town to another looking for work. She had syphilis in an infectious stage when they married, but she didn't know it. The soldier was sent to another base before their baby was born—a baby born with syphilis. He looked like a little wizened old man, covered with sores. That's how they found out.*

Eliot Ness and wife as they campaigned for mayor, October 21, 1947. *Courtesy of Cleveland State University's Cleveland Press Collection.*

Finally Ness suggested that soldiers and their girlfriends go to dances, read books together, go to the movies and dances, enjoy sports or have "just a good talk." The USO is mentioned as a proper place to meet nice girls, have a good time and not pick up a sexually transmitted disease. "But you must at least step inside the door."

What About Girls? did not mark a comeback for Ness, nor did it lead to any of the jobs he sought when he first resigned in Cleveland. Instead, he returned to Cleveland in 1947; made an unsuccessful run for mayor; was employed for a while at Diebold, primarily a manufacturer of safes and locks; and then moved to Coudersport, Pennsylvania, where he died in 1957 while finishing his self-serving memoir, *The Untouchables*. He had hoped to regain his former glory but instead died of a heart attack seemingly brought on by his hedonistic, alcohol-fueled private life.

The real tragedy in all this was the fact that Ness was truly untouchable by criminal special interests. He had an oversized ego, a tendency to take credit for far more successes than he achieved and to exaggerate his encounters with bad guys—just like

Eliot Ness campaign poster 1947. *Courtesy of Cleveland State University's Cleveland Press Collection.*

his professional enemy, J. Edgar Hoover. However, he made major changes in the police department, bringing in younger men who were often from neighborhoods where they had grown accustomed to watching officers shake down bars, pimps, prostitutes and others willing to pay in order to stay in business. These young men had been beaten by officers who were abusing their power, and those who had strayed into petty theft often were given a shopping list of items to steal for the beat officers and their supervisors. Some hated cops, and when Ness challenged them to put on the uniform themselves, getting rid of the types of men they hated and performing in a manner that would bring back neighborhood respect, a number of them did so. As a result, whatever his failings, the quality of law enforcement and community service improved greatly in Cleveland because of the legendary safety director.

Ness did return to Cleveland, or at least his ashes came back. They were taken to Lake View Cemetery, where a monument attests to his connection, but the ashes were dumped over one of the ponds.

ELIOT NESS CHALLENGES HARVARD (THE CLUB, THAT IS) AND HARVARD WINS

Ness was not lacking in courage…In 1935 Cleveland's Harvard Club (a gambling joint) flourished…The police chief and Ness went there with a warrant…As they approached—a machine gun was leveled at them…Alvin Karpis (later finished by the FBI) was at the trigger…Karpis told Ness it would not be advisable to proceed another single step….Ness laughed and kept advancing…nothing happened…except the demise of the Harvard Club.
—*Quote from Walter Winchell's nationally syndicated column, January 12, 1962, in which one item was dedicated to praising the late Cleveland public safety director. (Winchell did not mention that he had a part-time job as the narrator for the television show* The Untouchables *based on Ness's book and other semi-accurate stories. By the time Winchell felt he had to revitalize the alleged heroism of Ness, the show was heading toward its last season. It also had rarely shown the television Ness [actor Robert Stack] taking on investigations for which the real Ness, and the agency for which he worked, had any authority.)*

They were called carpet or rug joints, casinos that were somewhere between the backrooms of smoke shops where high rollers could win or lose thousands of dollars in an evening and sophisticated nightclubs offering food, liquor,
professional entertainers and the forerunner of Las Vegas–style gambling. The men who operated such places were in a finishing school of sorts, learning how to cater to high rollers, getting rich and unknowingly preparing for the day when they would help underwrite the new (legal) Las Vegas nightspots.

There were three primary Cleveland-area rug joints: Lake County's Mounds Club owned by Moe Dalitz, who would eventually move to Las Vegas; "Gameboy" Miller's Thomas Club (Mayfield Heights); and the Harvard Club in Newburgh Heights. Technically, Ness had no authority to go after any of the operations since they were as many as thirty-five miles from Cleveland. The Mounds Club was the gambling location of choice for many in the upper-income eastern suburbs like Shaker Heights and Gates Mills. However, Dan Gallgher, Arthur Hebebrand and James "Shimmy" Patton, the owners of the Harvard Club, countered their competition by establishing services for their clientele. Young men, many of whom later entered the rackets, drove cars to prearranged stops to pick up gamblers. A man seeking a night on the town with his lover or spouse could go to a pick-up location and be driven to the Harvard Club and then returned to the original drop-off point. Such service ensured that the customers often

Harvard Club, April 8, 1941. *Courtesy of Cleveland State University's Cleveland Press Collection.*

drank too much, gambled too long and stayed too late while losing money they could not afford to lose.

The Harvard Club became the focus of one of Ness's early crusades in Cleveland. He did not see gambling as a serious problem and might have ignored the Harvard Club, justifying his indifference because it was not in his city. However, the city was known to be corrupt, with law enforcement officers casual at best and taking payoffs at worst, while gambling in the city was a business estimated at $200,000 a week.

On January 10, 1936, a month after being hired as safety director, Ness made the move that created yet another legend in his own mind.

County prosecutor Frank T. Cullitan assembled a group of twenty constables, obtained warrants to enter the Harvard Club and pounded on the locked steel door in order to gain entry. The plan was to go inside and wreck the gambling equipment, putting the Harvard Club out of business. Instead, Shimmy Patton came out holding a machine gun and backed by heavily armed employees. Cullitan and the constables retreated to a nearby gas station and then called Newburgh Heights police for backup. They refused to cooperate.

Harvard Club, located at 4601 Harvard Avenue in Newburgh Heights, September 12, 1940. *Courtesy of Cleveland State University's Cleveland Press Collection.*

Cullitan was obsessed with gaining access, ignoring the events quietly taking place on the other side of the building. Patton and his partners were making plans to protect the club and their customers as Cullitan, desperate, called Eliot Ness.

The new Cleveland safety director was anxious to help Cullitan and was certain that he could find law enforcement officers who would assist. Instead, he learned the political reality of Cleveland. The mayor, Harold Burton, had been elected as a reformer, but he was a Republican reformer. Cullitan was a Democrat, and a Republican simply did not help a member of a rival party look good. Many local law enforcement officers also offered no assistance, having been paid by the gambling clubs ever since they opened for business. Finally, Ness went to a local police precinct where twenty-seven of the officers agreed to go with him as volunteers. (Ness was also a volunteer.) They could carry their weapons and assist in the raid, but they would technically have no arrest powers because they were out of their jurisdiction.

The one man who could legally assist Cullitan was "Honest John" Sulzman, the elected county sheriff. Sulzman was a firm believer in home rule within the county. Although the sheriff could legally help Cullitan since Newburg Heights was within his jurisdiction, Sulzman refused to go to the Harvard Club or allow his deputies to go there. He explained that he needed a request from the mayor of Newburg Heights, a man who had no interest in having so popular and profitable (through payoffs) an attraction shut down.

Ness arrived in the manner of a motion picture western. His "cavalry" consisted of ten officers on motorcycles, four plainclothesmen and twenty-nine uniformed patrolmen. Their weapons ranged from rifles and pistols to sawed-off shotguns, tear gas guns and billy clubs for close-in fighting.

Cullitan was startled by Ness's arrival. He wanted entry to the club. He wanted to shut it down. He did not want to witness a bloodbath because of his call for help.

Later, especially with a drink or two already consumed, Ness would tell what happened in a rendering more dramatic than the equally inaccurate Winchell account. The safety director claimed that he boldly walked to the barricaded door of the Harvard Club, knocked and announced, "I'm Eliot Ness. I'm coming in with warrants."

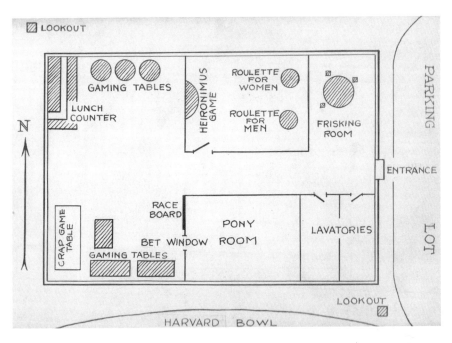

Harvard Club drawing of East Forty-second and Harvard. (The club changed its address over the years, the reason for some of the differences you may be noting.) *Courtesy of Cleveland State University's Cleveland Press Collection.*

Ness was known to practice jujitsu, the martial art that includes throws, kicks, punches and grappling moves. In the retelling, never recorded by any members of the press who were present, he positioned himself close to the door and let loose with a mighty kick. The steel was no match for the mighty Ness, and as it broke from the pressure of his shoe striking against it, he rushed inside, where he faced an armed assailant. Then, before the man could fire, the unarmed Ness proceeded to render him unconscious.

The truth was found in neither the Winchell column, written after Ness's death and resurrected in the form of actor Robert Stack, nor the alcohol-fueled memory of Ness himself. Instead, according to witnesses, Ness knocked on the door while the officers he brought from Cleveland stood alongside him. No one answered the front door, so they waited in the cold for an estimated five minutes or more for a response. Finally, a large, powerful-looking man in a tuxedo came to the entrance, looked with disdain at the men gathered in front of him and asked, "Who the hell are you?"

Ness flashed his badge and walked into the Harvard Club, which, by then, was mostly empty. Cullitan had started what must have been the slowest police

Gambling room in the Harvard Club, January 13, 1936. *Courtesy of Cleveland State University's Cleveland Press Collection.*

raid in history more than five hours earlier. There had been no standoff. There had been no shooting. Instead, while Cullitan, repulsed by the threat of violence, had sought help from everyone he could, Shimmy Patton and his clientele carefully dismantled the equipment within the barnlike former warehouse that had been turned into a popular gambling casino.

Most of the gamblers that night were area residents out for a good time and unconcerned about anything other than whether or not they would get lucky at their games of choice. A handful of hardcore gamblers was also there, determined to play so long as the place was open. And then there was Alvin Karpis.

Alvin Karpis was a professional criminal specializing in generally successful bank robberies and kidnappings, often working with Fred Barker, son of the notorious "Ma" Barker. The problem came in 1934, when Karpis and Barker decided that changing their appearance would enable them to function with reduced risk of being caught. They went to Dr. Joseph Patrick Moran, well known in the Chicago area as the man who took care of unwanted pregnancies and treated venereal disease for prostitutes working in brothels owned by Al Capone. He was discrete, and the facts that he worked for Capone and had spent time in Joliet State Prison in Illinois without giving up any of the criminals who hired him meant they could trust him. The fact that he was an alcoholic, they learned too late, meant that they should not.

Karpis and Barker paid Dr. Moran $1,000 to alter their facial features and to use acid to destroy their fingerprints. Instead, Moran painfully removed the top layer of skin from the gangsters' fingers and then cut their faces in ways that were painful and disfiguring without disguising their true identities.

Once the two men healed enough to function effectively, they took Moran to Toledo, Ohio, where they shot him and dumped him in a lake. Then Karpis made his way to the Cleveland area, enjoying life on the west side of the city and spending time at the Harvard Club.

Shimmy Patton used Karpis for two jobs. His primary work while on the lam was acting as security within the Harvard Club. However, he also was allegedly sent out to intimidate independent gamblers who set up high stakes games in the backs of smoke shops and other locations. These were small-time games, but such games could still represent thousands of dollars of business that otherwise would likely have gone to the Harvard Club.

Karpis, like the majority of the gamblers enjoying the Harvard Club when Frank Cullitan tried to raid the place, went quietly out the back door. During the time between Cullitan's first knock and Ness's arrival, money and gambling equipment were quietly removed. Only when Ness realized that men needed to be at all exits was the back watched by several armed officers, and by then there was only a handful of players inside, men who also were the only source of violence.

Despite Ness's claims of single-handedly subduing the owners of the Harvard Club, the one fight that did occur began when one of the gamblers who had stayed behind—either because he was winning when the raid began or because he was trying to win back his losses (his reasons for not leaving with the crowd were never reported)—pushed Byron "Shorty" Filkins, a photographer for the *Cleveland Press*. Filkins, no more than five feet tall, had been standing on a chair to get a better view of the almost empty club interior. The gambler, possibly fearing retribution from a spouse, did not want his picture taken.

Outraged by the incident, a reporter for the rival *Cleveland News* went into action. The man, known as "Big" Webb Seeley, slammed the gambler in the jaw, sending him sprawling across one of the crap tables.

Ness claimed another heroic act in bringing down the bad guys, but the press took a greater toll on the disreputable owners of the Harvard Club. And though the raid shut down the club for the night, Shimmy Patton continued its operation until the gamblers felt they might have better luck and fewer hassles at some of the area's rival rug joints. Only then was the Harvard Club closed.

Raid on the Harvard Club

Below is a partial report to FBI director J. Edgar Hoover concerning the raid on the Harvard Club. Notice that because the staff knew of Hoover's disdain for Ness, only the public safety director's position is mentioned, not his name.

From the May 12, 1936 MEMORANDUM FOR THE DIRECTOR Re: Police Corruption in CLEVELAND, OHIO
Federal Bureau of Investigation, U.S. Department of Justice

Referring to the close association between members of the Karpis-Barker gang and Arthur and Clarence Hebebrand and James "Shimmy" Patton, operators of the Harvard Club at Cleveland, Ohio, investigations by the Bureau have never shown exactly and in detail the manner in which this acquaintance was developed. Investigation has disclosed, however, as you know that Charles J. Fitzgerald was a member of the Karpis-Barker gang. We have learned that during the early summer of 1934, Fitzgerald visited with Cassius McDonald at Detroit, Michigan. Fitzgerald has admitted that he has known McDonald since 1924, when he first entered illicit traffic in liquor. It is safe, therefore, to assume that members of the Karpis-Barker gang became acquainted with Cassius McDonald through Fitzgerald. Investigation has shown that McDonald was intimately associated with Hebebrand and Patton. The investigation in Cuba and Miami, Florida, disclosed that McDonald corresponded with Hebebrand and Patton, therefore, in all probability, members of the Karpis-Barker gang became acquainted with Hebebrand and Patton and the Harvard Club through Cassius McDonald.

...John Brock has advised that James "Shimmy" Patton and Arthur Hebebrand formerly financed various jobs for Karpis and that at such times as Karpis visited Cleveland he contacted these two individuals. He further stated that Karpis arranges his Toledo contacts through an ex–prize fighter who is employed at the Harvard Club, the name of this individual being "Smoky" Sharkey Gordon.

Indicative of the close friendship existing between Fred Barker and Hebebrand and Patton is the fact that on November 28, 1934, while Fred Barker was living at Lake Weir, Florida, he wired a dozen roses from Ocala, Florida to "Art" Heavebrandt and James Paxon, c/o of the Harvard Club, 539 Harvard Avenue, Cleveland, Ohio. In wiring these flowers, Barker used the name of "T.C. Blackburn." It is interesting to note that when Arthur Hebebrand was later interviewed, he stated he recalled receiving flowers from Ocala, Florida, from a party named "Blackburn" but that he had no idea as to the identity of the sender.

Referring further to the close association between members of the Karpis-Barker gang and Hebebrand and Patton, [name blacked out] has advised that Alvin Karpis on one occasion informed him that he, Karpis, had been offered a proposition by certain gamblers in Cleveland whereby he, Karpis, could purchase an interest in an International Slot Machine enterprise for $5,000; that this syndicate had been negotiating with several large gambling syndicates in Europe for the purpose of establishing slot machines; that Karpis further stated that these men wanted him, Karpis, to travel to Europe and assist in the negotiations. Karpis at that time informed [name blacked out] that he, Karpis, was enthusiastic about this proposition and that he wanted to buy an interest at that time, but that the syndicate would not accept ransom money, which at that time was all he could offer them

With further reference to this matter, Karpis advised [name blacked out] that as soon as he, Karpis, was successful in changing portions of the ransom money, he would return to Cleveland and contact these people. [Name blacked out] went on to relate that Karpis had particular reference to Arthur Hebebrand and James "Shimmy" Patton and stated that Karpis had implicit faith in both of these individuals, in as much as they were the ones who tipped him off in regard to the contemplated raid on his place after [names blacked out] were arrested in Cleveland. [Name blacked out] further stated that it was his understanding that the premises occupied by Karpis and others in Cleveland were obtained through these individuals; that Arthur Hebebrand is reported to have an interest in a large real estate concern in Cleveland which bears his name.

Referring to the International Slot Machine racket, investigation has disclosed that W.J. Mitchell, mentioned hereinbefore, Clarence Hebebrand, a brother of Arthur Hebebrand, and William F. Fergus, did, in fact, go abroad together in July of 1935 and it is known that these individuals visited Rumania and Poland and in fact did establish certain slot machines in Rumania which were later withdrawn by virtue of the Rumanian government's disapproval.

On January 10, 1936, the Prosecutor's Office of Cuyahoga County, Ohio, raided the Harvard Club. The Bureau has made no independent investigation concerning this raid, but clippings from the January 11, 1936 issue of the *Cleveland Press* discloses that John Sulzman, Sheriff of Cuyahoga County, took no part in the raid; that the County Prosecutor enlisted the cooperation and aid of twenty-five private detectives and armed with search warrants endeavored to serve such warrants at the Harvard Club. They were met with forcible resistance, however, by Shimmy Patton, who threatened to "mow down" the raiding party with machine guns and held the raiding party at bay for six hours, during which time all the gambling equipment at the Harvard Club was moved away by trucks. It was finally necessary for the Safety Director of Cleveland to proceed to the Harvard Club, located just outside the city limits, with a party of policemen to gain entrance to the Club. This action was necessary because the Sheriff, when called by the Prosecutor's raiding party for aid, refused to send assistance even though his office was notified that the Prosecutor's raiding party had been threatened with machine guns. It is evident, therefore, that the proprietors of the Harvard Club were closely connected with politicians and those in power in Cleveland.

Eliot Ness? You Just Thought You Knew Him

WALTER WINCHELL

Hollywood is a place where they place you under contract instead of under observation.
—Walter Winchell

So where does Walter Winchell fit in with Cleveland's safety director? Ness made one more effort to return to the city that had accepted and fêted him until he became his own worst enemy, and during that time he was promoted for mayor, an election he eventually lost. With his successful career being revealed as something less than his image, Ness and writer Oscar Fraley teamed up to write *The Untouchables*, focusing on Ness's days in Chicago. Lucille "I Love Lucy" Ball and Desi Arnaz had formed Desilu Productions and bought the rights to the book, which was published just after Ness's death. They wanted to recreate the gritty realism of the 1930s and felt that a well-known radio voice from that era would make the perfect narrator. That was when they began negotiating with Walter Winchell, whose career was on the skids almost as badly as Ness's in his last days, though without the scandal of the alcohol.

Winchell was offered a sum he could not refuse—$25,000 an episode. It was not enough to restore his career as the nation's top celebrity gossip columnist, but it did make him quite wealthy. And as payback, Winchell's columns frequently praised Ness while always including even more positive words for J. Edgar Hoover. Ness, as the hero of a television show that Winchell narrated, put bread (and champagne) on the newsman's table. But keeping on the good side of J. Edgar Hoover, a man who collected files on everyone he did not like, regardless of any criminal activity, was critical to Winchell's future. Winchell did that delicate balancing act most effectively, and the ultimate beneficiary was the only partially deserving late Cleveland public safety director Eliot Ness.

Carrie Finnell's
Tassel-Tossed Tempest

C arrie Finnell came to Cleveland, looked around the city and decided to put on her clothes and stay a while.

Not that the management of the Empire Burlesque Theater (or the Columbia Burlesque Theater; supposedly equally reliable sources give conflicting theater names) minded. It was 1928, a time when a shoeshine boy could so profit from the stock market that he regularly tasted the finest bootleg gin and smoked the same Cuban cigars as his customers from Euclid Avenue's Millionaires' Row. And when men from both walks of life went out to experience Cleveland's night life—perhaps with friends, perhaps with the women who graced their arms, young ladies too beautiful, sophisticated and soft spoken to ever be mistaken for their wives—the Empire's Carrie Finnell was the frequent choice.

It was said that Carrie Finnell's countenance was not particularly attractive, though it is uncertain how many of her most ardent fans ever saw what she looked like above the shoulders. She was a circuit-riding gypsy, a burlesque performer at a time when the typical show was repeated for six days. The last show, late Saturday night, would end with the dancers and comics tossing their luggage in shared cars and racing to the next town, where they would perform, while the men who had been their audience, stirred by the beauty they just witnessed, left to find wives, girlfriends or willing professional women with whom they could share their recently stimulated enthusiasm.

To be fair, burlesque dancers like Carrie Finnell are a little like professional athletes who spend more time on the bench then on the field, the court or the gridiron. Each has risen to the top of her profession. Each receives a weekly pay that greatly exceeds what she can earn in what others would consider a normal job. Yet only a handful per team can be considered so outstanding that they seem like über athletes, playing at a level the ancient Greeks and Romans might have attributed to the son of a mortal and a god.

The difference among the dancers—the difference that gave Finnell the courage to take the stand she took—was that she had a skill as remarkable as that of the baseball pitcher who can accurately throw a curve ball with the speed of a fast ball, the basketball player who routinely sinks full-court shots and the football runner who moves seventy-five yards downfield while deflecting a half dozen tackle attempts by members of the opposing team. Had breast control and tassel tossing been Olympic events, Carrie Finnell would have had two gold medals every time she danced.

Other women knew how to put tassels on pasties and then gyrate their breasts to rotate the tassels. Carrie went one better. First there was her remarkable control. She might have been considered old for a stripper, and her critics derisively referred to her as "bovine," but when she stood topless, she could point her breasts in any direction she desired. Then, when her audience thought they had seen her entire act, she could set her tassels to spinning, each in a direction opposite the other, never losing a beat, never getting them entangled and in a manner rarely duplicated by any other dancer of her day. And it was because of that unique skill that she thought she could get away with a new approach to performing, one that would let her stay in town to dance long after the week's engagement was over.

Carrie Finnell walked onto the stage of the Empire Theater, gyrated to the music and removed one small item of clothing. "Come back next week and I'll take off more," she was reported to have told the audience, and though both she and the management were nervous about whether the idea would work, return they did—and not only that week but also the week after and the week after that.

To be fair to the other dancers and the baggy pants comics, Carrie Finnell developed her skills to a degree never before seen. The opposite spin was just one trick she had taught her extremely talented superstructure. Sometimes she would spin the tassels at different speeds, the left going faster than the right or the right exceeding the left. Sometimes she would leave on her blouse and then have one breast emerge, revealing a tassel that began twirling for attention while her other breast remained demurely unmoving behind the fabric.

It probably should be said that burlesque, as an art form, had changed in Carrie's day, though it was still a profession where dating customers was rare and having sex for pay was taboo. It did not have the dignity and respect as a training ground for cabaret performances, radio, television and movies that vaudeville enjoyed. But it did have a long history of satire and tweaking the nose of authority.

Burlesque was originally social satire that often featured plays with singers, dancers and comedians. It was Anna Held, the first wife of Broadway producer Florenz "Flo" Ziegfeld, who has been credited as the first actress to take off her clothes during a live theater performance in Los Angeles, twenty years before Carrie came to Cleveland. Not that the audience saw Held's nudity. The act in which she performed involved her taking off her clothes behind a screen so that she was silhouetted while singing "I'd Like to See a Little More of You." Held's show was in the Los Angeles Mason Opera House, and it was impossible to tell if she was really naked.

It was seven years after Anna Held's maybe/maybe not naked performance that a more shocking act was performed at the staid-sounding Pittsburgh Academy of Music. *The Girl In Blue* was the name of a show in which a woman known by the formal name Mlle. De Leon stepped onto the stage holding a parasol and wearing a full-length opera coat.

Mlle. De Leon barely had the audience's attention before she removed the coat and revealed…a leotard and tights. It was hardly a shocker by today's standards. The woman's figure might have been revealed, but her flesh was well covered. However, in 1915, the idea of a woman wearing tights was so shocking that she could be arrested. This extended to the circus, endangering female acrobats, who were forced to wear long skirts.

Carrie's act, though outrageous, either never violated local laws or local law enforcement simply joined the rest of the audience as she worked them so they would demand she stay. That first week, she removed just one item of clothing when she performed her dance throughout the day. The next week, she removed two items of clothing. The third week, three were tossed aside. Stories vary as to how long Carrie Finnell remained in Cleveland, though the most frequently cited time was approximately one year.

In 1938, late in Finnell's career, which had already spanned two decades, writer H.M. Alexander described her act:

> She stands there with her hands behind her back and by tricks of the muscles, flicks her breasts in and out of her dress. The finale of the act is executed to the tune of "Shave and a Haircut, Two Bits." On the "Shave and a Haircut" Carrie's breasts rapidly and in unison point left and right. On the "Two" they point down, on the "Bits" they point up.

Carrie Finnell's Tassel-Tossed Tempest

A more professional evaluation was given by dancer Ann Corio, who wrote:

She would start one tassel on one bosom slowly like a propeller revving up on a World War I plane. Faster and faster it would spin while its fellow tassel lay limp and neglected on the other bosom. Then, the other tassel would come to life. It would start spinning slowly, while the first tassel was at full speed. Carrie looked like a twin-engine bomber. Carrie could do anything with those tassels. She could make one go slow, the other fast. She could spin the left in one direction, and the right in the opposite direction. She could lie on her back and somehow keep the tassels elevated and twirling. She could attach tassels to her derriere and have them spinning every which way while the bosom tassels revolved merrily on their own.

It was an act so unusual that Finnell danced well into her sixties, her face and figure ridiculed by critics but her skills leaving them awe-struck.

Eventually, burlesque died off, not only in Cleveland but also throughout the nation, killed by radio, the movies, nightclubs and the emerging television. Cleveland's Roxy was the last of the local burlesque houses, and in 1962, when a high school friend and I fancied ourselves sneaking in on the assumption that we, at seventeen, were underage (the ticket taker did not care), the bill of fare was not as interesting as the audience. The star that night was the Fabulous 48, and she was no Carrie Finnell. She seemed to stare blankly into space, removed her clothing, turned her back to the audience and then placed her right breast under her left arm and her left breast under her right arm, after which she made sounds much like a hog caller. The baggy pants comics recited "The Shooting of Dan McGrew." And the rest of the women were less erotic than a Victoria's Secret display window. In between numbers, men roamed the aisles selling cold bottles of Coca-Cola and "provocative pictures from Paris."

As for the latter, exactly what the pictures might have been was never revealed. There were perhaps a dozen men in the audience that night, the last night for that particular show before new dancers and comics arrived. One elderly man in the front row, his face flushed and covered with sweat, had a handkerchief strategically placed over his crotch. Another man, sitting on the aisle, lusted after the man who sold bottles of Coca-Cola from a wooden carrier. He bought a cold Coke and then proceeded to watch the object of his lust move up and down the aisles while he stroked the bottleneck. The rest of the audience sat rather woodenly, none interested in whatever it was Paris had to offer.

Instead of burlesque, Cleveland joined the rest of the nation in introducing "gentlemen's clubs," places where there might be topless or scantily clad servers in tight tops—and always there were dancers. Some had style. Some were blatantly sexual. None had the special skills of Carrie Finnell, the woman who came to Cleveland and decided to put on her clothing and stay a while.

Leon Czolgosz

The idea that murder was an option for political change began in what should have been an innocent manner in May 1901. Spring had started warming the Cleveland air, and people who had spent the harsh winter months in relative isolation, going from home to job and back, were anxious to be out among others, sharing new ideas and developing new relationships. And among those who came to the city was eighteen-year-old Leon Czolgosz, the son of Polish-Russian immigrants who had settled first in Detroit and then just outside Cleveland, where they worked a small farm. The youth had never been a man of violence and apparently never owned a handgun. In fact, within his family, he was considered somewhat of an intellectual, having attended school a full five years before going to work.

The trip to Cleveland, a city that was like a second home for Czolgosz, was made in pursuit of a new, as yet unfocused direction for his life. He had worked the farm and worked in a wire mill, but an emotional breakdown returned him to the farm, where the repetitious physical labor gave him time to think about new ideas concerning the laboring man, politics and government. Among these was anarchy, and while he knew little of what it meant, he did know that the most famous advocate of the idea seemed to be Emma Goldman, who would be giving a lecture he planned to attend on May 6, 1901. Emma Goldman best described that day in her autobiography, *Living My Life*:

> *The subject of my lecture in Cleveland, early in May of that year, was Anarchism, delivered before the Franklin Liberal Club, a radical organization. During the intermission before the discussion I noticed a*

man looking over the titles of the pamphlets and books on sale near the platform. Presently he came over to me with the question: "Will you suggest something for me to read?" He was working in Akron, he explained, and he would have to leave before the close of the meeting. He was very young, a mere youth, of medium height, well built, and carrying himself very erect. But it was his face that held me, a most sensitive face, with a delicate pink complexion; a handsome face, made doubly so by his curly golden hair. Strength showed in his large blue eyes. I made a selection of some books for him, remarking that I hoped he would find in them what he was seeking. I returned to the platform to open the discussion and I did not see the young man again that evening, but his striking face remained in my memory.

Goldman had spoken in several different cities on a lecture/book-selling tour before she came to Cleveland, but the pace proved too grueling for her. The appearances were in conjunction with an organization that published the anarchist journal *Free Society* and had moved to Chicago. She went to

Emma Goldman in Cleveland during a ninety-day tour on March 16, 1934. She had earlier been deported and kept out of the United States for fifteen years on the grounds that she was a dangerous radical. *Courtesy of Cleveland Public Library Photograph Collection.*

that city from Cleveland, planning to leave from there for a vacation that would include visits with family members. However, before she could leave, a young man came to the home where she was staying and asked to see her. It was the same young man she had met in Cleveland, a youth who said his name was Fred C. Nieman.

As Goldman recalled:

> *Nieman told me that he had belonged to a Socialist local in Cleveland, that he had found its members dull, lacking in vision and enthusiasm. He could not bear to be with them and he had left Cleveland and was now working in Chicago and eager to get in touch with anarchists.*

Ironically, though Emma Goldman accepted "Nieman's" actions, the editor of *Free Society* had a very different idea. He was certain that the young man was a spy who was seeking the names of members and people planning acts of violence. What the editor, Abraham Isaak, did not realize was that the real danger was not Nieman the spy but Nieman the youth willing to kill for the anarchist cause, as he perceived it.

There were many reasons given by outside observers for the violence Czolgosz would eventually use against the president. None is certain for a number of reasons.

Reporters looking into his past were sometimes misled by the family, who called him their intellectual son. This was true only by comparison with his five brothers and two sisters. He was an avid reader but never finished elementary school. He was only able to find work in physical labor, where worker conditions were often extremely poor—the reason the union movement was gaining a hold in business.

Czolgosz was intrigued by the various labor movements, though he committed to none of them. He was also severely mentally ill, a condition that colored his actions. Some observers believe that he might have been developing schizophrenia when he first went to Cleveland to hear Emma Goldman; if true, that would make his irrational thoughts seem accurate. Certainly, he was increasingly seeing conspiracies where there were none and secret plots that were often ill defined, among other indications of extreme instability. He may also have experienced mania, for he seemed to believe that it would be his destiny to perform a great act that would change the life of the common working man for the better.

Czolgosz moved to West Seneca, New York, a Buffalo suburb, in 1901 and then returned to Cleveland at the end of the summer. Finally, on August

31, 1901, he again went back to New York, this time to Buffalo in the midst of the Pan-American Exposition. He stayed in the Polish section, an area familiar to him from similar places he had lived as a small child. From there, he sought work and, at some point, learned about President William McKinley's plan to visit the exposition.

On September 6, 1901, William McKinley stood at the Exposition's Temple of Music, shaking hands with men and women who had formed a lengthy line. The day was hot and oppressive enough to be distracting for the fifty security guards, who were not expecting major problems. In fact, even Czolgosz later said that the decision to kill was made at the last minute. (Later, there would be indications that Czolgosz considered killing the president in Cleveland but changed his mind, not wanting to disgrace his family in the region where they lived.)

Czolgosz later told the media that it was in the first day or two of September that he decided to kill President McKinley. He had not considered how to do it and, in fact, did not purchase the .32-caliber revolver he used until

William McKinley visiting Golden Gate Park. *Courtesy of Cleveland Public Library Photograph Collection.*

that morning, when he bought it for $4.50. Then he followed the president, looking for a place where he could shoot him. He thought that would be at Niagara Falls, which McKinley visited, but that proved a poor choice. He then continued following him until McKinley stopped to shake hands at the Temple of Music, where there was also a reception being held in his honor.

The shooting was a simple matter of coming close and firing two rounds into the president's abdomen. There were fifty guards present—apparently so many armed men that they became complacent. None noticed anything different when the man with a gun came forward.

Czolgosz was certain he had killed McKinley at that moment, though the president would linger for fourteen days. One bullet had struck the president's abdomen, and the other had struck his chest. Neither shot was fatal, and given more modern medical techniques, McKinley would have lived. Instead, the bullet that passed through the stomach wall and into one kidney turned fatally gangrenous.

Czolgosz might have kept shooting were it not for the heroism of civilian James Parker, who happened to be present at the moment the assassin fired. Parker, a waiter, grabbed Czolgosz and wrestled him to the ground, where the Secret Service agents were able to take control. They pummeled the would-be assassin until McKinley, still conscious and upset by the continued violence, shouted, "Be easy with him, boys."

The heroic actions of Parker were not released to the press at first because he was a black man, and it was felt that his actions showed him more competent and more courageous than the professionals who had failed to protect McKinley and had not responded until the shooter had been subdued by Parker.

Czolgosz was taken to Buffalo Police Headquarters, where he confessed to what he thought had been murder, not realizing his target was still alive. He said, "I killed President McKinley because I done my duty. I didn't believe one man should have so much service, and another man should have none."

The anarchist movement was briefly blamed for what happened, and Emma Goldman was arrested, along with some of her friends. However, she made it clear to the police and the media that though she was in sympathy with the desire to end government, she was horrified by the shooting of the president and would have nursed him had she been present. She also disavowed any connection with the former Clevelander who meant no more to her than any other curious young adults attending her lectures and reading her literature.

By September 10, four days before McKinley died, Czolgosz's madness was becoming obvious. He had been eating everything provided him when

William McKinley's funeral. *Courtesy of Cleveland Public Library Photograph Collection.*

first jailed but had stopped being interested in food. He also began pacing his cell and ignored personal hygiene. He did not change his clothes, and one reporter noted that the clothing and the underwear were the ones he had worn when he shot McKinley. The shirt was bloodstained, though from the beating he was given when arrested, not from the president's wounds.

The day the president died, Czolgosz was finally persuaded to put on cleaner clothing before being transferred to the Erie County Penitentiary. Justice was swift, the trial a foregone conclusion. On October 20, 1901, not two months after the shooting and barely a month after the president's death, Czolgosz was executed. Among his last words were: "I killed the president because he was the enemy of the good people—the good working people. I am not sorry for my crime."

Mrs. Chadwick Was
No Lady

Cassie Chadwick might be called the most socially prominent Cleveland heiress who never lived. Her father, it was whispered by all the "right" people, was steel magnate Andrew Carnegie, one of the two wealthiest men of his day. Her mother was unknown, though she was presumed to be as irresistibly beautiful as a siren's song since bachelor Carnegie's morals were of the highest order in that Victorian society.

The peccadilloes of Cassie's parents were a curiosity among the Cleveland elite, but being an illegitimate daughter brought disgrace only to the lower classes. The fact that she was the heiress to millions made Cassie as desirable in the city's mansions, private clubs and salons as if she had been the product of Immaculate Conception.

There were other advantages to inherited wealth. Access to cash was never denied. Bankers took Mrs. Chadwick into their private offices and provided her with loans for any amount of money she desired. They were always gracious, always kind and always solicitous about her well-being, all the while charging her interest rates far in excess of what was normal. It was Carnegie money, they seemed to reason, sums beyond comprehension. Besides, Cassie was such a genteel lady that she did not argue over the outrageous charges. She understood that the bankers' inappropriate behavior was the result of greed, and since she had no intention of ever repaying their loans, she knew she would not suffer at their hands.

Purveyors of upscale merchandise were more respectful of Cassie. They supplied her with the finest clothing, shoes, jewelry and accessories, always charging her a fair price for the quality items. The retailers only wanted a legitimately earned profit in order to ensure a long-term customer of such breeding. And even when payment was inexplicably delayed, there was little concern. Letting other customers know that one was helping to outfit the socially prominent Mrs. Chadwick was like a London merchant advertising that he was a purveyor of goods to the royal family. The price could be written off as advertising, and he would usually still come out ahead.

In addition to the things Cassie's wealth permitted her to acquire, she benefited in the press, where even her harshest critics muted their comments. Writers seeking her favor conveyed the image of Mrs. Chadwick as someone of great beauty, her body as sculpted as that of a showgirl and her wit and wisdom lauded as though she had attended the finest of finishing schools

Portrait of Cassie Chadwick in 1904. *Courtesy of Cleveland Public Library Photograph Collection.*

before given the standard "spoiled rich girl" tour of the continent. It was not until years after her death that more accurate physical descriptions appeared.

Cassie had both a speech impediment and was partially deaf. Her clothing was custom tailored, but her taste in style, material and color were enough outside the mainstream for her to be considered dumpy at best. A century after her death, in 1909, David J. Krajicek, a writer for the *New York Daily News*, described her as having been "corpulent and stern, she had a tight, unsmiling mouth, somber dark eyes and a nest of dull, dyed brown hair."

The two features that did not work against Cassie's appearance were her eyes and her demeanor. She would look directly at the person with whom she was speaking, her focus on them so intense that they felt themselves the most important person in her very privileged world. At the same time, there was a gentleness about her that made almost unthinkable the idea of questioning her personal history before she arrived in Cleveland. Cassie Chadwick was simply accepted for who she said she was, a lady fortunate enough to have been the "love child" of Andrew Carnegie and the adored wife of highly successful Cleveland physician Dr. Leroy S. Chadwick. No one, not even her husband, knew that Cassie Chadwick, arguably the most fascinating woman in Cleveland, did not exist.

ELIZABETH BIGLEY

In October 1857, Elizabeth Bigley was born to Daniel and Mary Ann Bigley of Eastwood, Ontario, Canada. The small-town couple had eight children in all, and keeping the family fed and clothed took more than one job. Daniel and his wife farmed a small plot of land in addition to his working as the boss of a railroad section gang.

Elizabeth Bigley was a reader and a dreamer as a child. Hers was not a life of hunger and privation as sometimes motivates those born into poor circumstances. Her family did as well as most of their neighbors and better than some. She had enough to eat, and the family could afford such luxuries as reading material, which Elizabeth devoured, always searching for stories about successful women in any endeavor.

Other children with similar interests might have considered opening a business, perhaps in one of the larger Canadian cities. Elizabeth seemed to have thought only about how to become a con artist, ensuring personal success through ill-gotten gains.

It was forgery that first intrigued Elizabeth Bigley. She learned about checks and how a bank would exchange them for real money if they were filled out correctly. More important, it was the banker's perception of the client that determined what funds would be made available, not a careful scrutiny and cross-check of a potential customer's true financial history. A man or woman who appeared to be well off but was impoverished would get a loan when someone who was wealthy but poorly dressed would not.

Elizabeth began practicing writing other people's signatures, though when exactly she first attempted to pass a forged document is not known.

Some reporters, writing after her death, suggested that she might have tried to pass a bad check for as much as $250 when she was thirteen years old. The stories, appearing in enough sources to possibly have been true, had her writing a letter stating that an uncle had died and she would be receiving a small sum of money. The forged notification of inheritance was good enough for an area bank to allow her to have checks for spending the money in advance of its arrival. The checks Elizabeth passed were genuine, the amounts nonexistent. She was arrested in 1870, told not to commit any more crimes and released. No one thought they could get a conviction against a thirteen-year-old girl.

Other sources say that the first scam came two years later, when Elizabeth was fifteen, and all the money came from selling a diamond ring she acquired from a neighboring farmer while she was still living at home.

The neighbor, a successful young man who had either purchased his land or inherited it from his family, fell in love with the teenage Elizabeth. She made it clear that she was a proper young lady, unwilling to go to bed with him until they were engaged.

Blinded by adoration, the farm youth mortgaged the land, bought Elizabeth a diamond ring and was promptly thanked as he desired. Then she returned to practicing forgery.

Elizabeth's first arrest came the year after her "engagement." One story says that she had been buying numerous personal items on credit from a local merchant, who eventually expected payment.

Another story had Cassie swindling several merchants, and when they became too demanding, she tried to cover her debts with a forged check for $5,000, an unimaginably large sum for a sixteen-year-old. Whichever story is true, and both may have been factual, the $5,000 forgery led to her arrest and subsequent acquittal on the grounds that she was temporarily insane.

It was when Elizabeth turned eighteen that she created the scam that would become the model she eventually perfected in Cleveland. Again acting with the knowledge that bankers were most amenable to providing large sums of money to men and women who did not need it, she became an heiress for the first time.

Elizabeth began the scam as she thought it might unfold in real life. First, there had to be a lawyer involved because a lawyer seemed to always be the person who handled wills and estates. He would also need to be from a large city and have been in the employ of a philanthropist.

Quality letterhead was obtained, and using the fictitious name and address of a London, Ontario attorney, Elizabeth notified herself that a philanthropist had died and left her an inheritance of $15,000. The letter looked official, and the amount was so large that it was presumed real.

Next, Elizabeth needed to present herself to the community in a proper manner so she could spend the money she had "inherited." Toward this end, she had a printer prepare business cards that were much like the calling cards of the wealthy and social elite. Hers read:

> *Miss Bigley*
> *Heiress to $15,000*

The scam was a simple one that took advantage of retail practices of the day. She would enter a shop, choose an expensive item to purchase and then write a check for a sum that exceeded the purchase price. Sometimes the merchants were happy to give her the cash difference between the cost of the item and the amount of the check, a crude version of a debit card transaction. Sometimes the merchant balked at the idea of removing so much money from his business when it would be at least twenty-four hours before he could begin having his bank process the check. Some questioned whether the young woman, who was said to appear even more youthful than her eighteen years, truly had enough money to cover the cost of the object. It was then that Elizabeth proudly handed the merchant her "business card."

The business card apparently worked every time. Why would the young woman have a card announcing herself to be an heiress if it was not true?

It is not known how long the scam could have continued had Elizabeth not became lazy. She should have gone to as many stores as possible in the course of a normal business day and then moved on to another city. Instead, she took a hotel room, let merchants know where she was staying and remained in London longer than the time it took for the checks to start to bounce.

The merchants immediately alerted the police, who, on Monday morning, raced to the hotel on the off chance that the "heiress" would still be in her room. She was, having packed her suitcases but not yet having checked out. She was promptly put under arrest, taken to the police station and presented to a group of merchants who had gathered to regain their money and property from the young thief.

(The early years of Elizabeth Bigley's life are presented here as accurately as possible. The problem is that she was committing her first crimes in Canada when her skills were still being developed, and there was little coverage of her arrests. Adding to this is the fact that seemingly reliable sources for facts can be contradictory. Was she born in 1857 or 1859? Both dates have been noted, though it is presumed that 1857 is correct since all the reports of her death in 1907 state that she was fifty years old. It is only after she left Canada for Ohio that the stories become consistent.)

Elizabeth's acting skills were far better than her forgeries at the time. She knew her appearance was odd, much younger than her years, so she took advantage of it. She scrunched her body, lowered her head and made herself look like a frightened, naïvely innocent little girl, not a scheming con artist.

The trick worked. The merchants decided to write off their losses rather than putting the obviously contrite child through further discomfort.

It was obvious that Elizabeth needed to work on her art. She had the heart and soul of a great con artist but her skills were still rudimentary. She returned to the family farm (no mention of any further relation with her neighbor has been found) and spent the next four years planning her future.

Elizabeth was twenty-two years old when she journeyed to Toronto. She dressed in her best clothing and brought with her a bank check of her own creation, a check that was for a substantial amount of money she would be transferring into a Toronto bank.

The fact that Elizabeth had no money and the check was a forgery did not matter. The check was duly deposited, and she felt herself free to spend the nonexistent funds while the deposited check was being cleared.

The big city of Toronto had financial institutions and businesses that moved faster than the other locations where Elizabeth had engaged in her scams. She spent the day she deposited the check going from business to business, buying whatever she desired. She took the merchandise to her hotel room, went to bed and discovered the police waiting for her first thing the following morning.

This time, there would be no escaping the law. This time, she found herself in court.

Elizabeth understood that appearance was everything. The fact that she looked like a small child the last time she was arrested gave her the impetus to try an insanity defense. While the prosecution presented the criminal case, Elizabeth stared off into space, laughed inappropriately, rolled her eyes, made odd sounds and generally presented the image of someone deranged.

The elaborate check-forging scheme had been done when Elizabeth was temporarily insane, the judge ruled. She would not go to jail. Instead, she would return to the farm.

Daniel and Mary Ann Bigley had had enough of their daughter's crimes. Another daughter, Alice, had married Bill York, a carpenter from Cleveland,

Ohio, and moved with her new husband to his hometown. Elizabeth soon followed, knowing her sister would help her resettle.

Elizabeth had no intention of imposing on her sister. She would stay in the newlyweds' home on Franklin Avenue only long enough to make adequate financial arrangements for a new business venture.

Alice and Bill may have thought Elizabeth was going to seek employment. Instead, she roamed their house, taking stock of all furnishings, from the chairs they sat on to the paintings on the wall. She determined their approximate value and then arranged for a bank loan using the furnishings as collateral.

Again, this is a period when the facts are uncertain. Some reports say that Bill learned of his sister-in-law's actions and threw her out of his house. Others say that this was one time when she knew to move out before matters got out of control. Either way, she kept the cash from the York furniture and used it to establish herself as the clairvoyant Madame Lydia DeVere.

She is also believed to have spent a short period of time moving from boardinghouse to boardinghouse, staying in each only long enough to get a bank loan for the home's furnishing as she had done with the Yorks. Whatever the case, she eventually settled in a home at 149 Garden Street owned by a Mrs. Brown. Madame DeVere had the entire first floor, allowing her a place to stay and to conduct business.

LYDIA DEVERE

Lydia DeVere had gone as far as she could on her own. She had a thriving business, money saved and money being spent for her services, and she probably could have continued with such modest success for many years to come. However, it was not enough. Lydia decided to become rich the old-fashioned way—through seduction.

The widow DeVere did not lack for suitors in those early months in Cleveland, though what may have drawn them to her side is uncertain. She had no interest in marriage for the sake of something as simperingly immature as love. Marriage was a serious commitment, and the man she chose had better have income equal to that seriousness.

Lydia did not realize that her determination to marry a man of means was easily matched by her creditors' determination to watch her business until they felt they could finally collect what they were owed. They were discrete, however, not letting anyone know they had observed the first successful swain since the neighboring farmer was gifted with her virginity.

Dr. Wallace S. Springsteen was a young Cleveland physician whose home was just down the street from the clairvoyant, at 3 Garden Street. He was new to his practice yet already had a reputation that made him of interest to the community. As a result, although the couple married in front of a justice of the peace on November 21, 1882, the *Plain Dealer*, one of the local newspapers, sent a photographer to record the event.

The newspaper story was read avidly by any number of merchants, as well as Lydia's sister, all of whom realized that Dr. Springsteen could be the source of their finally being repaid. Eleven days after the marriage, Dr. Springsteen returned to his home to find it filled with angry merchants (and one angry sister-in-law), all holding bills they expected to be paid.

Dr. Springsteen was no fool. He checked everyone's stories and realized that his bride was a liar, a forger and a thief. He divorced her immediately.

It was only later that it was learned that the good doctor was not so pure of heart, nor so smitten as it seemed. Madame DeVere explained to her paramour that she had an uncle overseas and, upon his death, had inherited a large Irish estate. It was the instant wealth the doctor envisioned for himself that caused him to rush Lydia to the justice of the peace.

The three months that followed Dr. Springsteen's discovery that his wife was a fraud played out like a drawing room comedy or slapstick farce. The creditors turned to the doctor for repayment of what they were owed, commandeering all his possessions, including the stethoscope he had the misfortune to bring home the day they arrived. Then, Lydia announced that her husband had promised her that if they ever separated, he would pay her $6,000.

The sum of money was outrageous, but so had been the idea that either of the two lovers might ever seek a separation from the other. Lydia was brokenhearted that it had come to a court battle, of course, but it was so obvious she would triumph that her lawyers loaned her large sums of money.

Lydia did triumph. By the time of the marriage to Springsteen, she was a far more accomplished con artist than in the past. She was divorced. There was no $6,000 promised. The creditors gained back nothing from her and everything from her soon-to-be ex-husband, who thought it better to settle than to have his own credit ruined. The lawyers were never repaid. Only Lydia made a profit from the sordid affair.

Some writers say that Lydia disappeared after the divorce, and in a sense they are correct. Lydia DeVere became the distinguished clairvoyant Madame Marie LaRose.

Among those who visited Madame LaRose seeking her advice about their futures was John R. Scott, a Trumbull County, Ohio farmer. He was apparently delighted to discover a woman of breeding and sophistication with an understanding of the farm life. They began dating, and she told him about the spousal abuse she had suffered in the past. It was not fair to John, but a man had treated her so badly that she was frightened for her future (which apparently she could not see with any certainty, despite her profession). When he proposed marriage, she agreed, though with one condition. She insisted on the protection of a prenuptial agreement.

The marriage between Marie LaRose and John R. Scott took place in 1883, and she apparently was quietly accepting of her new role, which took her away from Cleveland but not so far away that she couldn't return in less than a day. There were no stories of bank fraud or forged checks or similar crimes during this period. Either she worked with her husband on the farm or the good merchants of Trumbull County refused to prosecute.

Approximately four years after the marriage to Scott, Marie wanted out. She took the prenuptial agreement to a lawyer near the farm and then gave him a sworn statement that *she* had committed adultery. She asked the lawyer to file for divorce on the grounds that she had been unfaithful, an action that cut her off from her soon-to-be ex-husband's money and property. It may have been the one decent action she took in regard to any of the men in her life.

Clairvoyant Lydia Scott appeared back in Cleveland in 1886. This time, she worked from a Superior Avenue boardinghouse owned by a Mrs. Hoover, who left Cleveland a short while later. As with all things concerning Elizabeth, matters became complicated. First there was a change of name to Madame Lydia DeVere, which she felt sounded more professional. Other names were tried as well, including Madame Clinago, though why she kept changing identities within the same city is uncertain.

In the midst of all this, Elizabeth married a man named C.L. Hover (or Hoover; questions remain as to whether she used the Hover name during the marriage and adopted Hoover later or if records of the events used an incorrect spelling) by whom she had her only child, a son, Emil, who was believed to have been raised by her parents and siblings in Canada. Hover died in 1888, and Elizabeth returned to a number of scams, only some of which were documented.

Madame Lydia DeVere moved briefly to Toledo, Ohio, where she became a British citizen of substance who would be receiving large sums of money. She carefully described the estates that were to be her forthcoming inheritance, and the local citizens were delighted to make her their friend. They listened to her stories and offered her whatever money she desired to tide her over until her wealth could be transferred.

It was in Toledo that Elizabeth once again became greedy. A young man named Joseph Lamb first used Madame DeVere as a clairvoyant and then became so enamored with her that he asked her to serve as a financial adviser. This cost him $10,000, which she drained from his bank account. However, she was not through with him.

Lamb began living out a fantasy with Madame DeVere. The couple created a sexual version of a salon, a gathering in a wealthy person's home where fine conversation, music and literature were discussed, usually with wine and fine food. In the case of Elizabeth and Joseph, the evening started with a sexual romp and was followed by each reading poetry to the other.

The literary evenings were proof that Madame DeVere was somehow Lamb's soul mate. Elizabeth found in them proof that Lamb was naïve, immature and a mark waiting to be fleeced. She prepared a promissory note for several thousand dollars, the paper allegedly signed by a man identified only as a prominent Clevelander. Then she asked Joseph to cash it for her since she was from Cleveland and did all her banking there. She would have to travel back across the state to get the money if he did not help her.

Lamb could not stand the idea of being so long apart from the woman who was bestowing on him both her intellect and her physical favors. He cashed her note and then another and another.

Lamb had an excellent reputation in Toledo, and the bankers knew he would never work a scam. That was why, when they realized he was passing bad checks in several of their institutions, they totaled the amount taken fraudulently. It came to approximately $40,000, a very large sum of money at the time. Then they went to the police, and the ensuing investigation resulted in the arrests of both Elizabeth, who was tried under the name Betty Hoover, and her lover, Joe. He was the person who had passed the notes his lover created and thus he was potentially equally culpable under the law.

JAIL TIME

It was all for naught. There wasn't enough money in being a clairvoyant, at least not for Lydia. She returned to forgery, still not as skilled as she needed to be to stay out of trouble. Worse, she no longer was a sad-eyed innocent. She was arrested, tried and convicted. The judge sent her to a penitentiary in Toledo, Ohio, to serve nine and a half years.

Joe Lamb was surprisingly candid about what had taken place. He described first using Madame Lydia as his fortuneteller and adviser. He spoke frankly about the sexual affair, giving details as to when and where, though never how. Everyone was too proper to ask such a question. However, the jury had no doubts that Madame Lydia had used Lamb in ways he did not realize until the police came for him. They saw him as another victim of the female con artist and acquitted him on all counts against him.

Elizabeth did not waste her time in jail with penance for her life of crime. She had not yet achieved the success about which she had dreamed while a little girl reading about famous women. However, she still felt that the way to her fortune remained with crime. It just had to be handled with better planning and greater sophistication than in the past. She developed a number of ideas for new scams, and when she felt she had perfected them, she began a campaign for early release from prison. She had never used a weapon, never stolen, never hurt anyone and never threatened anyone or done anything terrible.

Elizabeth began a carefully thought-out letter-writing campaign to the parole board after serving her first three years. These were not forgeries. These were straightforward letters explaining the facts of her change, and the parole board agreed with her self evaluation. They sent the papers to Governor William McKinley, who signed them in time to have her released for Christmas 1893, three and a half years after she was jailed.

CASSIE L. HOOVER

It was Cassie L. Hoover who returned to Cleveland, the city she considered her home by then. She dressed conservatively. She spoke well. And most important for Elizabeth, there was no parole officer checking on her activities or revealing her past.

There had been stories of Elizabeth Bigley having worked in a London, Ontario or Toronto brothel. There is no record of such activity, but it would not have been out of character back when she was barely out of her teenage years. In any case, either in Canada or through conversations with fellow convicts, she apparently learned to run such a business, and it was to prostitution that she decided to turn next.

The idea was a simple one. The ever-so-proper Cassie L. Hoover opened a boardinghouse for young women. She also brought her son, Emil, back to Cleveland to live with her, adding to her image of respectability.

Cassie was careful about the women who worked from her boardinghouse. They appeared to have been independent contractors, each with her own clientele, rather than being house girls put on display for selection by the men coming by. The sex was more intimate and the facility's use almost like a dating arrangement, except that payment was always expected and Cassie always took her share as rent for the young women who were her boarders.

The use of brothels was not unusual for both married and single men at the end of the nineteenth century. Different cultures had different attitudes toward marital relations, with a number of them in the Cleveland area believing that sex was for procreation only. A wife was meant to breed, not enjoy the experience. Pleasure was to be derived from mistresses and prostitutes. However, such actions were always to be discrete and not discussed, including by the couple. More important, there was a double standard in regard to brothel and mistress use. Sex, even for pay, was a private act. Prominent citizens might use the same house of prostitution, but this fact could never be revealed.

Cassie recognized that whatever was an embarrassment to a wealthy man could be used by a savvy woman to acquire a portion of that wealth. She hired private investigators to get background information on her customers and, at times, to secretly photograph the men. Then, when she needed money and a customer was so prominent that he dared not object to any request, she blackmailed him, always keeping the amounts modest so she would not be reported to the authorities.

What happened next had the makings of yet another drawing room farce. The wealthy Dr. Leroy Chadwick, a prominent Cleveland physician, was a widower whose twenty-one-year-old daughter was away at boarding school. He lived quite properly with his ailing mother, but he was a relatively young man with certain needs that he no longer had a wife to meet. He quietly began going to the brothel owned by the genteel Cassie Hoover.

Cassie Hoover presented herself as a woman who ran a respectable boardinghouse for refined young women. The fact that when Dr. Chadwick mentioned a touch of rheumatism in his back, Cassie proceeded to reduce his discomfort with an impromptu (fully-clothed) massage—an action the doctor attributed to compassion and others considered seduction—did not alert the doctor to reality.

If there was any suspicion on Dr. Chadwick's part, it was allayed by Cassie's response when he noted that prior to her acquisition of the boardinghouse, the place had been known as an upscale brothel. Cassie may have been the brothel's madam, who entered the business with both eyes open, but she dared not belie her cover story to the wealthy widower. Rather than argue with the man, she fainted. It was the shock of discovering the embarrassing purchase into which she had clearly been misled that caused her to faint, she told the good doctor. Then she insisted he help her leave the establishment immediately lest someone think that she was a woman of ill repute who sold her body.

He apparently never explained why, if he knew it had been a brothel, he was visiting the day he met Cassie Hoover.

Exactly who Dr. Chadwick thought he would be marrying when he proposed to Cassie Hoover is unknown. She was single, of that he was certain. (Cassie's son, Emil, who had been living in the boardinghouse, was quietly turned over to a trusted young lady who worked there. It is probable that she never mentioned the boy's existence when Dr. Chadwick proposed.) She also wanted the privacy that could only be afforded through running off to get married. However, the minimal ceremony necessary, most likely performed by a justice of the peace, was held in Pittsburgh, apparently with neither friends nor relatives nor law enforcement officers in attendance.

And then the new life began! Elizabeth Bigley was the real Mrs. Leroy Chadwick, wife of the well-to-do physician and mistress of a stately two-story home just past the stretch of Euclid Avenue mansions owned by a succession of millionaires. The doctor's home would never be the primary focus of locals walking the street to see how the other half lived, but it would be more in line with what they could fantasize for themselves if they ever became at least moderately rich.

As Cassie had done with her sister and brother-in-law's home, she decided to make the Chadwick residence her own. This time, she did not mortgage the interior's rather somber furnishings. She had access to the doctor's healthy bank account, as well as whatever money she had set aside from her boardinghouse, so it only made sense to change the furnishings. Every piece. Without asking.

The Cassie Chadwick instant home makeover occurred on Christmas Eve 1897. Dr. Leroy Chadwick and his late wife had long been friendly with their neighbors, whose names were among the most prominent in the city—Mathers, Rockefellers, Hays, Hannas and others. Many of the neighbors were the first generation in their families to obtain great wealth, and they felt themselves in a similar social class with the doctor and his late wife. This new woman was something else, someone quite different. Her history was not known. Her family was not known. The schools she attended were not known. And in the world of the super rich—Cleveland's Millionaires' Row represented so much money that the homes were known throughout the world—to not have some sort of shared background was always suspect.

Cassie Chadwick cared about her neighbors but recognized that there was little she could do to make her mark on the part of Cleveland society that also had lower Euclid Avenue addresses. There were parties she and her husband attended because there were neighbors who still saw the doctor as a friend, as one of their own—albeit with less money—and including his new wife was the right thing to do. There were also people who either enjoyed Cassie's company or didn't mind it. And everyone in the neighborhood was intrigued by her unusual ways.

The Christmas 1897 home makeover was probably the most outrageous action those in the elite had ever witnessed.

The plan was a simple one. Cassie hated the furnishings in her husband's home. Everything was well made and expensive, but that was not unusual or unexpected. It was also rather somber, the wood and fabric dark and uninviting. It looked like the type of furniture designed for the prim and proper to sit upon day after day while contemplating morality, propriety and purity of heart, never smiling and feeling guilty for contemplating a respite from sobriety and a brief fling with happiness.

The walls, as was the custom, were adorned with portraits of Chadwick ancestors, each stiff and dull. Drapes were heavy and when closed against the sun would further darken the rooms.

Cassie wanted life, light and color, regardless of the cost. She began shopping for furnishings ranging from Persian rugs, hand-carved cabinets and tooled leather to elaborate chairs, couches and tables. Everything was ordered quietly, discretely and in a manner the good doctor would not know about until it was delivered.

There was a theater party on Christmas Eve that Cassie and Leroy were planning to attend. Cassie loved the theater and would eventually make trips to Manhattan to see the Broadway shows and other theatrical offerings, occasionally chartering a train so her friends could be treated to a weekend of shows. That night, the party was local, and the couple planned to be away for several hours, a time span Cassie found perfect to introduce the new furnishings.

As soon as the Chadwicks left their home, interior decorators, movers and craftsmen moved inside. The old furnishings were removed, and the entire interior decorations were changed. Little familiar was left behind, and that which was not removed was likely to be replaced in the weeks that followed when Cassie went on more open buying sprees.

The changes in the Chadwick home obtained the results Cassie had hoped for. She had gained the interest and attention of her neighbors, who were curious about what she had accomplished.

The furnishings were of three types. Some were the not unexpected possessions of the wealthy. Others reflected the idiosyncrasies of a fun-loving woman who was not afraid to show the lighter side of her personality. For example, there was what was called a musical chair, essentially a music box that played only when someone sat on it. She delighted in offering the chair, which looked like any other well-made piece of furniture, to a guest who knew nothing about it, enjoying their discomfort when the music rose like the sounds from a whoopee cushion.

Other "toys" were a perpetual-motion clock encased in glass and a full pipe organ in the home's music room. The latter cost $9,000 and equaled or exceeded the quality found in many theaters and churches.

Dr. Chadwick soon discovered that his wife considered the home's new furnishings to be little more than a stage set for the life they would share. She began shopping both in Cleveland's most expensive boutiques and in

The Chadwick Library, where she kept a beloved glass clock. *Courtesy of Cleveland Public Library Photograph Collection.*

other cities where there were specialists she admired or knew would be admired by her neighbors. This meant custom-designed diamond jewelry from Toronto, custom-made hats and clothing from New York City, furs from Cleveland, sculpture from the Far East and furniture handcrafted in Europe.

Leroy Chadwick was a highly successful man in his day, but he lacked the income to maintain the lifestyle his new bride expected to enjoy. What he did have was real estate, property that made him quite wealthy in good times and was a limited resource when real estate values were depressed.

In the years before he was widowed, Chadwick apparently handled the buying, renting and selling of his real estate holdings. He was cautious in bad times and made excellent money in good times, all in addition to what he earned from the practice of medicine.

The doctor's exhaustion from the stress of his wife's death, getting his daughter through school and all the other concerns in his life led him to happily turn over the management of his property to his new bride. She ignored sound business practices, ignored the downturn in the real estate market and reduced the doctor's net worth to practically nothing.

However, before Leroy Chadwick could do more than feel uneasy about what was taking place, Cassie began the largest and most successful scam of her career. She was going to maintain her lifestyle and keep her husband happy with the funds to which she had access as an heiress.

CASSIE CHADWICK, HEIRESS

Cassie Chadwick ultimately settled on two key elements to make the scam work. The first was that she had to choose a victim who was so successful and so well known that he would likely never be aware of her scam. And the second was that she had to return to the banks in such a way that no matter what she might tell them, no matter how humble her demeanor, there would be no question in their mind about her wealth.

Cassie carefully plotted the actions she would take. Her husband apparently remained so besotted of her that he was not yet challenging her spending sprees or complaining about what she was doing to the family's finances. Perhaps it helped that at last Cassie was being accepted in Cleveland society, since many of the neighbors wondered just how wealthy she might be. Perhaps the couple's continuing to live in the slightly more modest circumstances was their eccentricity. Perhaps this Chadwick woman could buy their homes and their furnishings and hire away their servants if she so chose. It was better to be nice than sorry.

Helping spread the rumors that were helping Cassie's image was an attorney named Dillon, a friend of the doctor. He apparently handled basic business needs and was not sophisticated in finance. However, he was considered extremely competent and was highly respected among the elite. He was also a gossip who could be counted on as surely as the supermarket tabloids would be a half century later. Cassie knew that she could rely on the attorney's mouth to deliver all the news that was fit for titillation.

Dillon was delighted to enjoy a free trip to New York City and was not concerned with the fact that he had been told nothing of the reason for Mrs. Chadwick's possibly needing his expertise. The fact that she had booked a suite of rooms in the expensive Holland House for her stay added to her image in the lawyer's mind.

(Some sources indicate that she did not take Dillon to New York but planned her trip based on when he told her husband he would be going and where he would be staying. In that way, she could "accidentally" bump into the attorney and take him along with her as witness to the seeming veracity of what was about to unfold. Regardless which story is accurate, Dillon accompanied Cassie the day she went to see her "father.")

New York was serviced by hansom cabs, each of which had a specific route. Cassie signaled to one that traveled the length of Fifth Avenue, New York City's equivalent of Cleveland's Millionaires' Row. She did not give a destination, just had the coachman take them until they were approaching Fifty-ninth Street, at which time she asked him to stop. Cassie explained that she would only be a few minutes, that Dillon should remain in the cab and that the driver would be taking them back when she returned. Then she alighted and walked purposefully to a mansion the lawyer learned was the home of Andrew Carnegie.

The reality of the mansions owned by the wealthy was that they were almost like small towns. The staffs were large and many of the rooms were used only for parties and intimate concerts for a few hundred close friends and the like. The actual living quarters were likely to be separated from the rest of the house so that various trades people could come and go, dealing with the staff and never seeing or being seen by the wealthy owners. Cassie was admitted without question as anyone would be. What Dillon could not see was whether she was greeted warmly, as a friend returning after being away for a time, or professionally, as a delivery person might have been.

Mr. and Mrs. Andrew Carnegie. *Courtesy of Cleveland Public Library Photograph Collection.*

Cassie was well dressed enough that the butler who answered the door believed the story she told him. She explained that she was hiring a new staff person, had done her advertising in New York and was following up by checking references of the applicants who seemed most promising. One of them, and she provided the butler with a name she invented on the spot, had claimed to have worked in Andrew Carnegie's home. She was stopping by to confirm the statement.

The butler was indignant, not with Cassie but with the woman who had given a false reference. He assured the doctor's wife that the woman had never been employed there and that Mrs. Chadwick should definitely not give her a job.

Cassie thanked the butler and left, slipping a large brown envelope from her coat in such a manner that, from Dillon's angle, it seemed that she was carrying something she had been given inside the mansion.

Dillon may not have known much about who lived where in New York City, but the cab driver had told him that the home Mrs. Chadwick entered, a seemingly welcome visitor, belonged to the fabulously wealthy Andrew Carnegie. He was eager to have Cassie explain what she had been doing there. He also wanted to know about the envelope, though he had the good sense to not request an immediate explanation for that.

As the cab returned down the avenue, the lawyer pressured the wife of his client and friend. There had to be more to what had taken place than what was obvious or she would not have brought him along.

Cassie was a far better liar than when she was young, and as would be discovered shortly, she was also a far better forger. Slowly, with what seemed great reluctance, Cassie said what Dillon already knew—that the mansion was the home of Carnegie. Then she added one bit of information, the reaction to which would take her to the top of Cleveland's society. Carnegie was her father.

The story that was related was a sad one, and though it would have been easy for the lawyer to check the facts even before they left the city, he was too deeply moved by compassion and an urgent desire to gossip. Cassie's mother was unknown to her. Her father wanted to keep her from negative notoriety, but he freely acknowledged Cassie. In fact, he had arranged for her to have the documents in the envelope, documents she had created herself with the skills she seemed to have been honing for almost her entire lifetime.

Most of the papers were unimportant. What mattered were two notes, each of which assured Cassie of great wealth from her generous "father." That they were dated fairly far in the future did not seem out of line. She was a woman naïve in the ways of the world. It was important that she not be taken advantage of, even by so seemingly honest a man as Leroy Chadwick, MD.

The notes, signed by Andrew Carnegie himself (or so they seemed), were for $250,000 and $500,000, respectively. Each would make her the equivalent of a multimillionaire in today's money. Each was dated January 7, 1904, approximately two years away, and once that date was reached, there would be twelve more months to wait before receiving the money: "One year after date, I promise to pay to Cassie L. Chadwick $250,000 [the $500,000 note had similar wording], with interest at five per cent."

(To understand the magnitude of Cassie's crime, take the dollar amount she was fraudulently obtaining and multiply it by twenty-five to see the amount in today's dollars; $100,000 at the end of the nineteenth century would have the buying power of approximately $2.5 million today.)

Know all men by these presents that I, Andrew Carnegie, of New York City, do hereby acknowledge that I hold in trust for Mrs. Cassie L. Chadwick, wife of Dr. Leroy S. Chadwick, of 1,824 Euclid Avenue, City of Cleveland,

County of Cuyahoga, and State of Ohio, property assigned and delivered to me for said Cassie L. Chadwick by her uncle, Frederick R. Mason, in his lifetime, (now deceased), which property is of the appraised value of ten million two hundred and forty-six thousand dollars ($10,244,000), consisting of 2,500 shares of Great Western Railway stock of England and Wales, valued at two million one hundred thousand dollars ($2,100,000); 1,800 shares of Caledonian Railway stock of Scotland, valued at one million one hundred and forty-six thousand dollars ($1,146,000), and bonds of the United States Steel Corporation of New Jersey, bearing 5 per cent interest, of the par value of seven million ($7,000,000) dollars.

Dillon, now a trusted confidant of his friend's wife, began looking through the other papers. They were all securities valued at a total of $5 million. They were, in a sense, an inheritance that would ensure a future more comfortable than almost anyone had ever enjoyed. All were there. All were properly prepared. And all were not to be cashed until several years after the death of the elderly Carnegie.

While others were amazed at the short-term wealth, ignoring the fact that the proof of the notes would take three years if no one checked back with Carnegie, the scam was actually based on the $5 million in securities. Cassie would borrow against it because the people with the ability to loan her any sums she wanted chose to believe that no one would be so outrageous as to create an elaborate paper trail of lies.

THE SCAMS

Cassie's scam involved large sums from several financial institutions—Oberlin, Ohio's Citizens Bank; Cleveland's Wade Park Banking Company; New York's Lincoln National Bank; and Oberlin College's endowment fund—and smaller sums, though never less than $10,000, from what may have been a dozen other banks. The facts that her home address was within the area known as Millionaires' Row, her husband was a physician and she moved money around in such a manner that she was paying off the early loans with later money all helped her actions seem legitimate. The facts that she was willing to pay higher than normal interest and apparently provided private financial incentives to some of the bank officials all helped her continue the scam.

Various writers covering Cassie Chadwick's story provided differing details concerning how the scam moved from bank to bank. What is certain is that Cassie started by taking what were, for so wealthy a woman as she was supposed to be, small loans of no more than $1,000. She would take several loans from more than one bank, quickly paying off the first with the money from the second, paying off the second with money from the third and so forth. This was similar to a Ponzi scheme, except it was never meant to provide her with profit. Instead, because of the bankers charging higher than normal interest, the loans cost her money, a situation she anticipated when planning her crimes. The paybacks ensured that Cassie Chadwick became known as a woman who could always be trusted to meet her financial obligations.

Cleveland's Wade Park Bank was the base of Cassie's operations. It was there that she placed her undetected counterfeit promissory notes for $7.5 million. At least one other note was retained for use in Oberlin, where Charles B. Beckwith, president of Citizen's National Bank, was one of Cassie's first victims, both professionally and personally. The bank loaned Cassie a total of $240,000, and Beckwith—some reports say along with his cashier, a man named A.B. Spear—loaned her another $100,000 from his/their personal account. Beckwith also became one of the first people, aside from Dillon and Cassie's husband, to learn Cassie's secret about Andrew Carnegie. Since she could show a note with his signature, albeit one whose value was several years away, there was no question about who would ultimately be responsible if there were any unforeseen problems. What went unsaid was that the total capital stock of the bank was only $60,000, one-fourth of the loan Beckwith approved.

The scam became most complex in Oberlin, where the bank was the smallest and least sophisticated of her victims. She convinced the president that she wanted to give an endowment to the college, though what her connection to Oberlin College or the community of Oberlin itself might have been was never said. Ultimately, C.B. Beckwith gave Oberlin the money as Cassie directed; Cassie then needed to pay back Beckwith. She took another loan from Wade Park Banking Company, sending some of the money to Beckwith and depositing the rest into an account with Lincoln National Bank. A loan from Lincoln National Bank paid off the loan she acquired from Wade Park Banking, and then a new loan from Wade Park Banking paid off Beckwith.

The endowment scam came when Beckwith made it clear that bank regulations prevented Citizens Bank from loaning her any more money. However, the college had an unused $50,000 in its endowment fund. The endowment could be used to make loans in ways that would provide a fair profit for the fund. Cassie had proven herself so credit worthy and so prudent in her repayment of loans that the school's endowment fund was turned over to her for whatever use she required.

Cassie Chadwick was committing her crimes in an era of slow-moving paper and few credit checks. No one seemed interested in checking on her background or her business deals because so much money and so many prominent people were involved. As a result, the scam took on a life of its own, permeating every aspect of society as few in Cleveland were privileged to know it.

Cassie and Dr. Leroy Chadwick joined the Euclid Avenue Baptist Church not far from their home. The church was run by the Reverend Charles Eaton, pastor to John D. Rockefeller, who became rich through his Standard Oil Company. Eaton, in turn, had a brother, John, living in Boston and working as an attorney. Attorney John Eaton, in turn, had a client named Herbert D. Newton, who worked as an investment banker in Boston.

The Boston scam was typical Elizabeth Bigley. It involved forgery, lies and greed, the latter on the part of the seemingly honorable investment banker. He was happy to provide the Cleveland woman with a loan and even happier when he was able to give her a check from his business for $79,000 and a personal check for $25,000—$104,000 in all. He was even happier to establish repayment terms such that she signed a promissory note for $190,000. Elizabeth, in her role as Cassie, said nothing about the outrageous interest. She was a lady, after all, and she had no intention of repaying the investment banker who had shown himself to be no gentleman. It goes without saying that had he treated Cassie fairly, she still would have had no plans to repay him.

The occasional personal loan, provided both because Cassie was a good credit risk and because it might win the favor of her "father," was often higher than the bank loans. Elyria, Ohio's Savings and Deposit Bank provided Cassie with $10,000, but a Pittsburgh steel magnate, perhaps acquainted with Carnegie, gave her $800,000.

Retailers throughout Cleveland were the real recipients of Cassie Chadwick's largesse. The banks lost their money but the merchants were paid in cash before their goods left their stores.

Cassie understood that she remained the most talked-about wealthy Clevelander to not be accepted by the social elite, so for a while she tried to buy her way into society. Many a merchant was shocked when Cassie acted outrageously to impress others. Certainly there were the furs and jewels, but when one music store had a grand piano she liked on display and another twenty-six in the warehouse, she bought them all. She told the clerk that they would serve as presents for her friends.

The problem with Cassie's generosity was that that it simply wasn't done by women of the social class into which she was trying to be accepted. Come to dinner in the home of Cassie and Leroy and you would find an unusually expensive gift, perhaps of jewelry, on your napkin as a gift from your hostess. Go to work for the Chadwicks and you would be given discards of clothing so fine that today the elite would be buying them from upscale resale shops. You would be given cash bonuses that might exceed your pay. You would be treated, if not like a guest, certainly more like a family member than an employee.

Everything was overdone, a fact the doctor was believed to have understood, though there is no record of his comments. Cassie interwove diamonds in her hair. She had diamonds adorning her dinner dress, which was made from the finest available fabric. Everything about the evening was slightly overdone. As the years passed, she proved she had access to more money than the rest of them, wore it surprisingly well and yet seemed a bit overwhelming. Her every action demanded notice, acceptance and friendship, but the reality seemed to be that she was primarily noticed. She made a few friends, but she never was so fully accepted in Cleveland society as the doctor had been before his second marriage.

Dr. Chadwick undoubtedly knew the lack of respect that existed for his wife. Still, he not only loved the woman, but he also saw how her financial expertise rebuilt his personal fortune. She even went so far as to help others through the establishment of the Cleveland Loan Company.

It was November 24, 1904, when the life of Cassie Chadwick started to unravel. All Herbert Newton had ever desired was an unfair profit from a legitimate loan to the wealthy doctor's wife. Instead, it had become obvious that she had no intention of repaying him. That was why he filed suit one November day in the Federal Court of Cleveland. He requested that he be paid $190,800, and to prevent Cassie from removing and hiding her great wealth, the suit requested that Iri Reynolds of the Wade Park Bank continue to hold the $7.5 million in the bank's possession.

Elizabeth Bigley had learned one important lesson in her years as an evolving con artist and that was to move boldly, openly and in a manner a guilty person would never do. That was why she immediately traveled to New York City to once again meet with her "father."

Much of the new trip was as it had been before—the expensive hotel suite, the hansom cab, the trip down Fifth Avenue. The lawyer was not present, however, and riding behind Cassie was a carriage filled with several of her creditors. These were all wealthy, prominent men of the world of high finance, but none was in the league of Andrew Carnegie, and all were afraid of confronting Carnegie's wrath. That was why they stayed outside the mansion, watching Cassie enter as though her visit were routine and welcome. Thirty minutes later, she emerged from the mansion with new promissory notes, created in the manner of the successful ones from years past, their total being $1 million. Everyone would be satisfied. All investments were safe. Or so the doctor's wife hoped they would assume.

Instead, the bankers did their due diligence, as they should have done in the past. They made contact with Carnegie's office, asking about his illegitimate daughter, a woman named Cassie Chadwick, and each was told the same thing. Andrew Carnegie did not have an illegitimate daughter, nor did he have any children. He had never heard of Cassie Chadwick, and he had certainly never signed any promissory notes. For the previous several years, the bankers had been working with fraudulent documents.

In the week that followed, while Cassie stayed in the Hotel Breslin in New York, a city she felt would be more sympathetic to her presence than if she returned to her home at the end of Millionaires' Row, Iri Reynolds was ordered by the court to bring in the sealed envelope of Carnegie promissory notes. Reynolds, proud of his personal integrity and certain he had made no mistakes with either the bank's money or his own funds, provided the judge with $7.5 million in worthless counterfeit paper. Then, realizing how badly everyone had been misled, he sat down at a table and wept. The less emotional judge ordered the New York authorities to arrest Mrs. Chadwick.

SOJOURN IN THE TOMBS

On December 8, 1904, the *Cleveland Plain Dealer* reported:

> *In default of $15,000 bail, just the sum that she paid down in cash for a gem that tickled her fancy in the heyday of her financial whirl, Mrs. Cassie L. Chadwick was led to a cell in the Tombs at 9:02 o'clock tonight. All day her counsel had made frantic efforts to keep her out of prison. Yet, after a twelve hours' search for money, Mrs. Chadwick had to acknowledge defeat.*
>
> *It was a moment of anguish to Mrs. Chadwick when her counsel, Phillip Carpenter, returned to the office of Marshall Henkel in the federal building shortly before 9 o'clock. She raised herself on her elbow from the couch and gazed at him without uttering a word. He shook his head. Mrs. Chadwick*

trembled. Her face twitched convulsively and it seemed that she was about to faint. Her son, Emil, jumped to her side and threw himself on her knees.

It is known that Mrs. Chadwick appealed to all from whom perhaps assistance might come in her hour of need. Messages were sent to Cleveland, where she had been lavish in giving presents to friends. No answer was received. Mr. Carpenter tiptoed from the room, his face haggard.

But even in this hour of utter rout Mrs. Chadwick's courage flashed up. She would not ride in a public conveyance to prison. She whispered to her son, and he hastened out to order a carriage. It drew up and Emil notified his mother that all was in readiness. Mrs. Chadwick appeared, leaning heavily on the arms of her son and Marshal Henkel. Too weak to raise her feet, Mrs. Chadwick shuffled slowly to the elevator, striving in vain to check her sobs. The party passed through a double row of curious people to a carriage which was in waiting on the Broadway side.

They were driven directly to the Tombs. Arriving there Mrs. Chadwick was half carried up the steps and into the building. Warden Flynn met the party, and after the usual preliminaries had been attended to the woman asked permission to have her nurse [Freda Swanson] remain with her. This was denied, the warden saying that she should have no privileges not allowed other prisoners.

Mrs. Chadwick gave a handbag and a few trinkets to the nurse, and whispered some instructions to her son. Marshal Henkel formally turned his prisoner over to the warden, and she was taken to the matron's room. She asked to say good night to her son, and the lad eagerly rushed to his mother and, wrapping his arms about her, gave her a long embrace. Then she was led away to the inner office, where her pedigree was taken and she was assigned to a cell. The son and the nurse entered a carriage and were driven to a hotel.

The arrest led to hardships that were unexpected, such as being treated little better than a common criminal. The Associated Press reported:

Mrs. Chadwick dined at 7 o'clock tonight (December 8) in Marshal Henkel's office under conditions in strange contrast to the manner in which she lived at the New York hotels. [Cassie had been avoiding arrest by switching hotels, though always staying in luxury—the Holland House, the New Amsterdam Hotel and the Hotel Breslin—each time seeming to want to elude the Secret Service agents who were making certain she did not leave New York prior to her arrest.] *Her dinner consisted of an orange, a ham sandwich and a piece of cake, brought to her by her son from a Broadway lunch counter. She lay on a hard leather couch in a room filled with desks, chairs and file cases. A deputy marshal stood watch while her nurse took the meager lunch from a paper bag and peeled the orange. Emil sat by in silence and ate a few bites of a sandwich, and the nurse dried her tears long enough to taste the lunch counter fare.*

The following day, Cassie Chadwick had her son see the marshal and learn the procedure for returning to Cleveland. As it turned out, all she had to do was appear before the same commissioner who had set her bail the day before and then provide a hand-written request. However, returning to Cleveland would change several factors, the most important one being that she was more likely to lose. In New York, her lawyers explained, she could have the case tried in the criminal branch of the United States Circuit Court in that district. She could bring in witnesses and mount a defense that would likely succeed. Nothing awaited her in Cleveland except further criminal charges and the disdain of the locals.

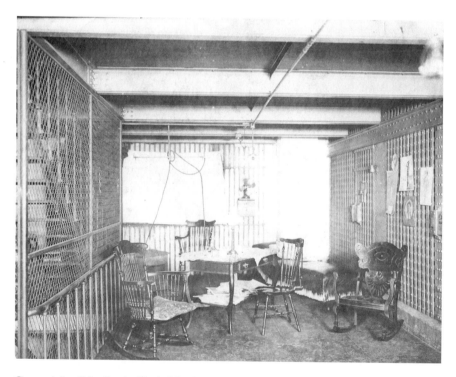

County jail cell for Cassie Chadwick where she was provided with a reception area, date unknown. *Courtesy of Cleveland Public Library Photograph Collection.*

Legal Wrangling

I was informed today on what I am certain was excellent authority that the notes presented by Mrs. Chadwick and signed "Andrew Carnegie" were genuine, and were signed by Andrew Carnegie, not the steel magnate, but a close relative of his. I am certain that will be the defense of the people now accused of forgery in connection with this case.
—*Judge Francis W. Downs, Binghamton, New York, December 8, 1904*

While the legal issues for sending Cassie back to Cleveland were being resolved, she began working with the media to gain public opinion in her favor. On the evening of the ninth, she met with a reporter from the Associated Press who had been investigating stories that were gradually being reported in one newspaper or another throughout the United States. The arrest was becoming a major news event. Either Cassie Chadwick was the illegitimate daughter of the wealthiest man in the United States or she was a fraud who had obtained massive sums of money over the previous several years. Ultimately, the numbers would be staggering—as much as $19 million at the time, close to a half-billion dollars in today's currency.

One of the questions involved Elizabeth's sister, Alice Bigley York, who told the press that she was the sister of the woman calling herself Cassie Chadwick. Mrs. York was living in San Francisco when the arrest occurred.

Cassie understood that complete denial could result in her coming across as a liar. It was better to admit to a portion of the truth so that her accuser became suspect.

Emil had already stated that he knew Mrs. York as Aunt Alice. "I have stayed at her house and I was taught as a boy to call Mrs. York's boy my cousin," Emil answered when questioned. Then a written statement from Alice York was shown to Cassie, who commented, while lying on a couch in the U.S. marshal's office:

> *I have not read all of it, but I will leave it to public opinion and to refined and educated persons what conclusion they might draw when one sister makes a statement like that against the other sister. Tonight, in the presence of the marshal, I said to my little boy, "Emil, have you read Aunt Alice's statement?"*
>
> *He said, "Yes." I was in hopes he had not and I said to him, "What do you think about that, dear?" and he replied, "It is nothing more than I expected from her."*

The reporter then asked, "Is Mrs. York your sister?"

And Cassie replied, "No, she is neither my sister nor my half sister nor my sister-in-law. We were raised together."

"Will you say anything about the statement that you are Mme. Devere?" asked the reporter, a man who had obviously heard from Cassie's sister about some of the aliases she had used in past scams. However, Cassie was too skilled a liar to be caught reacting in any way that might work against her. This was also why her attorneys did not want her returning to Cleveland. She was a skilled liar who might fool the people in a city where they could not imagine anyone creating the stories she had told about her background. Cleveland had already seen her many incarnations, no matter how skillfully she continued to lie.

> *I have made absolutely no statement about this Mme. Devere business from beginning to end. Out of justice to my little boy I would not do it at the present time. I don't think that any responsible person would pay any attention to a statement made by Mrs. York. If I had a sister or a brother who was in trouble, no matter what their past might have been, if I could not do him or her good I certainly would shield him or her from harm. It is unkind and unfair for any person to give such a statement for publication and I question whether she gave it unless she was paid for it. There must have been some inducement.* [Cassie did not mention the fact that during the short time she lived with her sister and brother-in-law she had borrowed money against everything of value they owned and then did not repay the bank. Their loss would be reason enough to tell the full story of her sister's lies.]
>
> *Everything will work its way out all right for me and I don't want to say anything against Mrs. York at all. I shall make a statement here in the very near future and also one in Cleveland. The newspapers possibly have written up a great sensation, but I wish you to say that Mme. Devere's whereabouts and everything else in connection with this case will be shown in a very short time.*

The reporter then asked Cassie about the notes from Andrew Carnegie. "Whatever is said about those notes must be said by my attorney, Mr. Carpenter."

Finally, Cassie sought to explain the financial problems that led to her arrest and questions about the soundness of the banks with which she had been doing business. Again, she wanted to control her image, especially knowing that what was quoted could have an impact on the charges against her and any trial. She explained:

Mrs. Chadwick Was No Lady

Mr. Newton brought this lawsuit against me on Monday. On Tuesday and Wednesday they had a run on the Wade Park bank. Of course that frightened the people because of the enormous amount of the lawsuit, $210,000. That was a very large amount in a little city of only about 400,000 inhabitants. That amount of money attracted attention. The depositors of the Wade Park bank became alarmed that the bank was going to be ruined, when in reality I only owed the bank $17,000 and it was one of the best and most conservative banks in Cleveland.

No, I am wrong. It was Friday the run commenced on the Wade Park bank. Then, following that, one of Mr. Newton's notes was in the Oberlin National bank. On Saturday evening the Oberlin bank opened to receive deposits, according to its custom, from 6 to 8 o'clock. The depositors in that bank read in the Penny Press *the sensational story that I owed the Oberlin bank. They rushed into the bank on Saturday night and, instead of making deposits, commenced to draw their money out. It was a small country bank and only had on hand $11,000 or $12,000 in cash. The other money belonging to the bank was in the Cleveland banks and, it being Saturday night, they were closed up. The depositors drew heavily that night. Someone came in with a check. I think it was for $2,800 or $3,800, and they did not have money enough to pay. Therefore they had to close the bank. They could not open it again and notified the bank examiner. They said they could not demand the loan against me because I was down here in New York. The story had gone out that the bank had failed and it was too late then for anything to be done.*

Mr. Miller of Canton, the bank examiner, had to be sent for. He got to Oberlin on Sunday and they went into conference Sunday afternoon. Mr. Miller found the bank was in such condition that it had to be closed, because the depositors had become so exercised about the reports they all drew out and nothing would quiet them. If it had only happened differently the bank would not have had to fail because the obligation would have been paid.

"I would not like to live a minute if I did not think I could pay these poor people back," she said shortly before ending the interview."

There were other details that would be revealed later, including the fact that Mrs. Chadwick had been planning an escape, perhaps to a new identity, all funded by $100,000 in genuine money she was wearing in a belt around her waist when arrested. Not that she admitted her plans. She would later be quoted as stating:

Public clamor has made me a sacrifice. Here I am, an innocent woman hounded into jail, while a score of the biggest business men in Cleveland would leave town tomorrow if I told all I know. Yes, I borrowed money, but what of it? I will even admit I did not borrow in a business-like way. I wish now I had followed old rules a little closer. But you can't accuse a poor business woman of being a criminal, can you?

In a sense, Cassie was right. Between the blackmail operation she ran from her boardinghouse for allegedly respectable young women and the unethical contracts bankers gave her to gain more of their wealth, she could have ruined the biggest names in Cleveland. That was not her style, however.

JUSTICE

Ultimately, justice was served in rather odd ways. Beckwith came to visit Cassie in jail, his attitude toward the scam still one of disbelief. As he was quoted telling her, "I am not convinced you are a fraud." However, whatever he thought, the stress overwhelmed him. He had a heart attack when he first learned how badly his bank and his personal finances had been damaged. After seeing Cassie, he had mentally deteriorated, perhaps from the heart attack or small, unnoticed strokes; perhaps from some other cause. However it happened, he became so depressed that he shot himself in February 1905. Had he lived, he probably would have gone to jail as well because his actions were improper enough for him to be considered part of Cassie's conspiracy. Also implicated was bank cashier A.B. Spear, who served five years in prison.

Andrew Carnegie was both intrigued by what had taken place and embarrassed by the hurt caused by his name. He attended Cassie's criminal trial in order to learn more about the woman who had conned so many while pretending to be his daughter. He then quietly arranged for Oberlin College, which had lost $50,000 thanks to Beckwith's mishandling of the endowment, to receive three times that much. The $150,000 that was quietly provided the school was used to build a new library. As for his decision to not personally charge Cassie with a crime, he explained, "Wouldn't you be proud of the fact that your name is good for loans of $1,250,000 even when somebody else signs it? It is glory enough for me that my name is good, even when I don't sign it. Mrs. Chadwick has shown that my credit is A-1."

Goodbye Cassie Chadwick

Dr. Leroy Chadwick, shocked by the truth concerning his life with a woman who did not exist, divorced her. He then took his daughter on a trip to Europe so they would be out of the country when Cassie went on trial.

The trial ended on March 10, 1905, the jury taking five hours to find her guilty of conspiracy against the government (Citizen's National Bank of Oberlin was a federally chartered institution). She was fined $70,000—$30,000 less than she had been carrying in her money belt at the time of her arrest, though whether she was allowed to keep the rest of the cash is not known. She was also sentenced to fourteen years in prison. She was moved to the Ohio State Penitentiary in Columbus on January 1, 1906, and was allowed to keep trunks full of clothing and furs. However, even having personal items she loved did not change the reality of her confinement. She found sleeping increasingly difficult, lost thirty pounds in weight and was so unpleasant to the warden and prison staff that the woman who once seemed able to charm anyone was often intensely disliked.

Cassie was not well and began preparing for her death. She had money hidden in Canada and instructed Emil where to find it and how to distribute it. She also arranged to be buried in Holy Trinity Anglican Church Cemetery in her home community of Eastwood, Ontario, Canada.

Cassie Chadwick. *Courtesy of Cleveland Public Library Photograph Collection.*

The days before Cassie Chadwick's death were as outrageous as so much of her life. She was transferred to the infirmary after collapsing during one of the visits by her son. She apparently had several small strokes. During her last days, she was provided with whatever food she desired, and she chose rich delights she had not enjoyed since she was a free woman two and a half years earlier. According to the doctors, it was the rich food that took her life on the day of her fiftieth birthday.

And so, Cassie Chadwick, a woman who never existed, had perhaps a greater impact on Cleveland society than any woman who ever lived.

Maurice Reedus Jr.:
Sax in the City

Few Clevelanders recognize the name Eddie Smoot, and perhaps fewer still know the name of Maurice Reedus Jr. Eddie Smoot was a kid with a dream shattered by the vagaries of life. Maurice Reedus Jr. was a kid who didn't think he dared to dream until Eddie Smoot entered his life. And while Smoot is now a trivia question related to Cleveland's music history, Reedus, though little known by name, is arguably the most familiar face in downtown Cleveland. It is impossible to go to more than one or two sporting events, productions in the theaters in Playhouse Square, the fast-food restaurants on East Ninth Street between Superior and St. Clair, the Euclid side of East Fourth Street, Public Square at midday or any number of other downtown locations without hearing the notes from his ever-present saxophone.

The Reedus story started with Smoot. The latter was eighteen years old, an age when some youths give up on life and others discover they can genuinely live the dream they have been secretly harboring. Smoot was a master of the conga, essentially an oblong bass drum that looks and usually sounds like it belongs in an elementary school rhythm band. Most players, including those performing with Cleveland's top Latin musicians in the 1950s and 1960s, could do little more than use their hands to make a variety of repetitious beats, the primary difference among them being whether they were loud or soft.

Eddie Smoot was different. He worked the drumhead with a lover's caress. Let him touch the surface and instantly the stretched membrane begins to vibrate, a cat contentedly purring. The beat was added, matching the music being played by the other musicians, then taking off like a colt racing ahead of a stallion, dropping back to nip at the older animal's heels and

Maurice Reedus Jr. *Photograph by Ted Schwarz.*

then moving alongside, matching stride for stride, before racing ahead once again. Smoot had the taunting playfulness found among top jazz musicians challenging one another's improvisations in after-hours joints where they would cut loose until well after sunrise.

Eddie understood what he was accomplishing with every performance on local television amateur programs popular in the era, in clubs catering to Cleveland's Hispanic community, at wedding receptions and anywhere else he could get a gig. Tragically, Eddie also had an ego that demanded what proved to be a misguided flamboyance. He decided to make his congas as beautiful to look at as the music he created was to behold. He took paint and glitter, "pimping" the wood in anticipation of his next gig.

Exactly what happened next is no longer remembered with any certainty. There may have been an explosion. There may have been a spilling of the liquid. Whatever happened, the glitter-laden paint was suddenly in Eddie's face and in his eyes. One moment he had the world. The next moment the past was over and the future would have to be molded by the man who forever would be known as "Blind Eddie Smoot."

Whatever grief and frustration Blind Eddie endured after the accident, he did not let it prevent him from two achievements. The first was dating some of the most beautiful women in the city, at least as far as the other kids his age could tell. And the second was his determination to teach what he knew to boys being raised in the projects, often by single parents or couples whose minimum wage jobs forced them to work long hours away from home. The boys would become musicians, playing the conga in a way no one in Cleveland had ever heard from anyone other than Blind Eddie before his accident.

Maurice Reedus Jr. was one of the boys being raised in Garden Valley, a name implying a loveliness and peacefulness that the brick and fencing did not match. Cleveland's projects were designed to provide homes for a massive number of people in a minimum amount of space. Many of the problems—drugs, alcohol, truancy from school and the like—came from the tension of too-close quarters, too little recreation and too many people whose limited skills meant they were the last hired and the first laid off as the economy changed.

The Reedus home was different. Maurice Reedus Sr. was a comedian and saxophone player who turned professional in the early 1950s after the Korean War. Opportunities for black performers were increasing, but top stars of the day—Nat Cole, James Brown and others—often had to perform for segregated audiences. James Brown was the most prominent of the entertainers who rebelled against the system. He never played an auditorium where blacks could not come in.

"The [musician's] union never did anything for you though they'd say they would," Reedus Sr. reminisced shortly before his death from cancer.

All they wanted was their dues. Here in Cleveland you'd make $10, $11, $12 for an evening, they'd come around and take two or three dollars for your dues. They never got you anything so we always tried to dodge that cat.

When acts came to town, they'd hire the white cats to play behind the acts so we didn't get anything.

I remember once we had our dues paid up and we went to play a club called The Ritz in Youngstown. It was a theater but I guess the mob must have had that because we played there a week over New Year's. We did weekends on the front and on the back. We finished on a Sunday and were to come back on Monday to get our money. Then the padlock was on the thing.

We talked to the union and they were supposed to get the money. Never heard from them again.

Maurice Jr. never saw the harsh realities of the music business for his father. This was the time when payola was big, the record companies giving money, stereo equipment and other items of value to the disc jockeys in order to ensure regular airplay of whatever record was being promoted. This was also a period when the union and some of the club owners or managers would demand kickbacks under the table. The musicians would get paid an agreed-upon amount, a contract would be drawn up and everything would be straight until the money was paid. Then a percentage was expected to be quietly returned.

The jobs that were available to Maurice Sr. were glamorous events to his son, who was making his way through school. There were sock hops, for example, school dances where the kids kicked their shoes off in what was usually a corner of the gym and then danced to often big name singers brought in by a local disc jockey such as Joe Finan of KYW (now WKYC). Della Reese, Dinah Washington or some other big name act would be performing, and there would be Maurice Sr. on the bandstand, blowing his sax, providing the background for the greats of the era. The stars usually got their money. The local musicians hired for backup rarely did, despite a contract with agreed-upon fees.

The older Reedus persisted. Music was his love, no matter where he had to work for a day job when music gigs (or fair payment) became scarce. He eventually worked his way around the world as a sax player for musicians such as organist Jimmy Smith, Sonny Stitt, Johnny Shines, Nancy Wilson, Dionne Warwick, Della Reese, Billy Eckstein, Lou Rawles, Hank Marr and Jimmy Garrett, among many others. His absences also led to his succumbing to the traditional temptations of the road, where loneliness frequently led to affairs. He cheated on his wife and the marriage ended.

"I always wanted to be just like my father," said Maurice Jr. "I wanted to walk like him. I wanted to talk like him. I wanted to wear the same clothes he wore. He was just so cool. I used to think he was the coolest man in the world. I think that way today, too."

It was Blind Eddie Smoot who provided the transition from troubled youth to professional musician. Maurice Jr., born in 1953, was eleven years old when Blind Eddie Smoot entered his life. Garden Valley had been one of the more enlightened housing projects when it was built, and there was a neighborhood house on the grounds. Various people from the community came there to provide whatever they thought might be of benefit to the residents—educational programs, information about nutrition, medical help and the like. And among the people who decided to work with the residents was Blind Eddie Smoot. He explained that he was going to put together a musical group featuring young boys. They didn't have to have any musical training. Everything they needed would be provided. They just had to be serious about learning and performing under Smoot's direction.

Maurice Reedus Jr.: Sax in the City

As Maurice Jr. recalled, it was 1964, he was eleven years old and "there were 25 little boys [auditioning], and out of 25 he wanted six." Maurice made the cut and soon was playing conga drums in the group Eddie Smoot and the Courageous Young Men.

> *We called ourselves the CY Boys, and Eddie Smoot would stand in front of us and direct us. A blind man. We had three conga players, two guys on maracas and a bongo player. And we'd sing and we played. We did all the Motown sounds, but we did it on drums.*

The boys also had a signature ending song that Smoot meant as much for them as their audiences. The song was "I'm Going Back to School."

But staying in school was not easy for Maurice. He learned to pronounce the words in his schoolbooks, but he couldn't make sense of them. The same was true for music. There had been no written music from Blind Eddie Smoot.

Smoot adapted his teaching and conducting style to his recent disability. He always had at least one assistant in the practice room the boys used, though the assistant was most helpful in keeping track of the boys when they tried to wander off. Blind Eddie Smoot had no problem hearing the developing skills of each of the Courageous Young Men. He was able to guide them, not only on an individual basis but also with the sounds they made as they learned to play together for concerts. He also visited them in their homes, making certain they practiced, worked at their studies and were becoming professionals worthy of respect.

Maurice thrived as a musician under Smoot's guidance. His low self-esteem was countered by the fact that he had become part of the CY Boys when so many others had failed. He did not have to read music because his mentor could not read the music. Instead, he developed his ability to hear the music and to understand how to be most effective, both solo and in a group. He became intensely competitive, wanting to excel for Smoot, and for his father, and to hide his own limitations.

Maurice was an almost complete academic failure, a fact his mother, with whom he lived after his parents' divorce, never understood. The problem of dyslexia was understood even when it had no name, and many educators lacked the training to work around the disability when teaching. More frustrating for both mother and son was the fact that no one ever explained to them that this was not a form of retardation or brain damage. In fact, Dr. Toby Cosgrove, the surgeon who became head of the Cleveland Clinic, was and is dyslexic and went to school during the same era as the young Reedus.

"I thought I was stupid," Maurice recalled. "I thought I was worthless. I couldn't read books. I couldn't read music. I became the class clown and the teachers thought I was just trying for attention."

What Maurice and his teachers did not realize was that he was dyslexic, as lost in the world of books and sheet music as he was brilliant in the world of sound. Alternative ways of teaching had been developed in England's pre–World War II Montessori schools, among other places, but if his teachers understood, they had no interest in helping a black kid from a broken home. (Both parents remarried, and all the adults in Maurice's life made certain that their relationship problems did not interfere with their relationships with Maurice.)

It was as one of Eddie Smoot's conga players that Maurice was first introduced to the world of show business. Most schools had talent contests in those days, and many of them offered money, trophies or a chance for gigs at the birthday and graduation parties of students whose parents came to the talent shows.

In addition to sock hops and other teen activities, Cleveland's airwaves were filled with local and national music shows. Perhaps the most famous was Herman Spero's *Upbeat*, a new type of rock 'n' roll television program. Previously, the national standard had been *American Bandstand*, where host Dick Clark would have one performer and ten dance numbers. The only variety in the music came when watching week after week. By contrast, Herman Spero's concept was to have just one dance number and ten performers. His son, David, who held cue cards and handled other tasks on the set at WEWS Channel 5, remembered that the mix in any given week was as varied as the Temptations, Tommy James, Johnny Cash, Duke Ellington and others. The show was so different that other cities and networks imitated the concept with such programs as *Hullabaloo* and *Shindig*. In addition, there was the largest music program in the nation, *Soul Train*, which featured acts once dismissed as performing "race music" yet dramatically influenced the musical experience of a mixed audience. It was into this world that Blind Eddie Smoot introduced Maurice Reedus Jr. and the other Courageous Young Men from the projects.

The congas were Reedus's first instrument, and several decades later, he is still unable to walk into a music store displaying a set of congas without taking his hands to the surface, his eyes focused not on the drums or the business in which he is standing, but at a point in the past, as though the sounds of his hands are a bridge leading from where he started to who he has become and a comforting presence to accompany him into tomorrow. Yet despite the obvious hold, it is the saxophone that defines who he is today.

THE SAX

Maurice Reedus Jr. was in sixth grade when he picked up the baritone sax. Although he would grow to be well over six feet tall, young Reedus had only just become big enough to handle the instrument when he entered Rawlings Junior High School.

Sharon Reedus, Maurice's older sister, played the clarinet. The Rawlings music teacher encouraged the students to try instruments, learning to play them for the band. Maurice started with the clarinet in order to hide his limitations. He would seem to look at the sheet music when the band rehearsed, but he was actually watching Sharon's fingers, mastering the instrument by memorizing her finger positions and the sounds her instrument was making. He became so skilled that the band director never knew he could not comprehend what he saw. Then, when he started the saxophone, he had no idea how accomplished he had become.

Six months after joining the school band, Maurice began learning to play the saxophone. His mother took him to the music department of Higbee's, the department store that was headquartered in Terminal Tower in downtown Cleveland. Maurice Reedus Sr. may have been his son's inspiration for becoming a professional musician, but it was his mother's relationship with the Higbee Company that enabled him to get his first saxophone.

There had been a time when radio station WHK occupied space on the twelfth floor of the building that was once the second tallest in the world. The station never paid rent. Instead, all its advertising, whether on air or on billboards, included "WHK, on top of Higbee's at Public Square."

WHK moved out in 1951, leaving behind space that had high ceilings, sound-proof rooms and facilities that would lend themselves to a number of purposes, including being a location for selling both radios and television sets, which were just beginning to be popular with consumers. It was finally decided to call it the Higbee's Music Department, where everything related to entertainment—record players, radios, television sets, sheet music, musical instruments—was sold. There was a concert hall where groups could both practice and perform. In addition, there was the Higbee Preparatory School for Music, and it was to this department that Maurice was taken when he was ready to learn to play the saxophone.

The School for Music allowed parents to have children try an instrument, including taking a lesson, with no charge. The idea was to give the parents a low pressure way to see if their children were serious about an instrument.

The concept behind the instrument sales was to create a satisfied customer who would return again and again for more music, more advanced lessons and perhaps a more expensive instrument. There was also a performance hall within the large department that attracted famous touring groups, providing both a service to the public and a chance for extensive free publicity from the local media.

Reedus was one of the students who benefitted from Higbee's. His mother was able to rent his instrument and to get him free lessons and practice sessions until she was certain he wanted to master the sax. Then she was able to buy the instrument a few dollars at a time.

OPPORTUNITIES

Cleveland was a city where music was seemingly everywhere and jobs were plentiful. Kids who put together a competent music group could expect to find work during the rites of passage of others their ages or older. Families would hire them for birthday parties and religious celebrations. There were amateur contests, and promoters such as Gene Carroll had a weekly television show featuring young singers, dancers, musicians and the like. There were school dances and even after-hours clubs. The latter were places where you could go to drink, pick up women, sometimes gamble and listen to live music. They opened after the licensed bars and nightclubs had to close, and they were often still providing entertainment when most people were on their way to work.

The clubs were technically illegal, though unless there were problems with drunks and violence, the police generally left them alone. A number of them hired skilled teenage musicians to play, providing the members of the group respected the fact that they were underage and would not be allowed to drink alcohol.

The Courageous Young Men would never play in any place that could prove embarrassing or get the youths in trouble. However, as Maurice grew older, other kids, talking about their experiences, exposed him to the greater possibilities for his playing.

Maurice was anxious to increase his musical skills, and though he rarely talked about it, what he really wanted was to be just like his saxophone-playing father.

FOREIGN BLUE

Reedus's first band was a group of high school kids who called themselves the Foreign Blue and became the youngest band ever to play inside Robert Harris's Sir-Rah House on Lee Road. The club, legendary in those years of lingering racism in nightclubs and bars offering entertainment, was the place where top talent routinely appeared. Every major black musician who performed in Cleveland knew he or she would be welcome even if they were turned away from other clubs. The fact that a group of kids might convince the owner to let them appear, and then become regulars, was previously unheard of.

The audition for Harris, like the audition process for the other clubs where Maurice and the others played, was simple. They would go into the club before it opened. The owner would usually be sitting at the bar, overseeing the last minute cleaning and setting up before the place opened for business. The band would set up its instruments and start to play. If the owner and the servers liked what they heard, they would get the gig. Then, once they had proven themselves by playing for a night or two, Maurice would introduce the fact that he also had a comedy act that he could do between sets. And the success of that act could lead to solo gigs with just the comedy.

Looking back, Maurice credits Little Johnny Britt, one of their group whose sound, style and vocal range matched that of Michael Jackson. This was a time when the Jackson Five were performing to sold-out audiences throughout the world, and listening to Britt was the same experience as listening to Michael. What he does not consider was the fact that each of the boys in the group was extraordinarily talented, that Foreign Blue was equal to many of the top adult acts. He, like the others, had been discovered by Harris, who insisted on Maurice doing a comedy act as a regular part of the show and, occasionally, on his own.

Foreign Blue became almost a house band, playing on its own and as a lead-in to major acts. They may have been high school students, but they performed in the Sir-Rah House on Wednesday, Thursday, Friday, Saturday and Sunday. They were stars who had been discovered by Harris but had yet to recognize their own talent when they looked in the mirror.

COMEDIAN

Life changed dramatically for young Reedus when he met Terry Stubbs during a summer school session. Stubbs, who attended Kennedy High School, was another kid with a dream. He was trying to become a singer/songwriter, and toward this end he had become a part of a singing group of slightly older boys. John (Sly) Wilson, Charles (Slick) Still and Mark (Wicked) Saxton had formed Sly, Slick & Wicked in 1970. Two years later, Terry replaced Mark and recommended that Maurice be hired to be part of a small backup band. There was no audition.

Maurice and the other kids hired to be part of the backup musicians were all young, most barely out of high school, and they began meeting regularly to rehearse in a club called the Funky Broadway at East 131st and Broadway. This was also where Reedus began showing the comedy skills he had developed with the act he had started refining at the Sir-Rah House.

There had been a number of years when top comedians were limited in the clubs where they could perform because of racial prejudice. However, Maurice Sr. had traveled the same circuit and studied the acts of people like Redd Foxx and George Kirby, both just beginning to become successful in what had been white-dominated clubs. Maurice Reedus's father began incorporating the Redd Foxx style of humor in his act, and young Reedus was allowed to stay backstage where his father performed. Soon he was memorizing his father's act and taking it to clubs on weekends:

> My best feelings on the stage came when I was doing comedy because I had everybody's attention; everybody laughed. I felt like really on top of the world because people were listening to me and I was making them laugh. And I couldn't believe it.

It was 1970 when Maurice Reedus Jr. first went on stage to tell jokes. It was at the Sir-Rah House on Lee Road, and he was little more than a kid himself. He was terrified that no one would laugh or that he would forget his lines. Still, it was a dream he had had for five years, ever since he was in Columbus with his father and attended a show where his father told jokes:

> I was fourteen. I never knew my daddy told jokes. I just knew he played the saxophone. He stood on that stage and the audience was laughing. I never saw that before. They were laughing. They loved it and I knew I wanted to do that, too.

Maurice Reedus Jr.: Sax in the City

Maurice Sr. was an established professional, much to the surprise of his son. He would change his voice, exaggerate his movements and use odd facial expressions—whatever it took to get the audience laughing with him.

Those first times on stage were all imitations of the material Redd Foxx and his father had been using. Maurice listened to recordings, practicing the lines, the phrasing, the pauses and inflections. It was more than comedy by rote. He learned the jokes the way he learned music, mastering the style that always brought laughs. "I knew if I could get it just right, I'd have the adults laughing at me," he said. "I was scared of forgetting the lines or forgetting the order for the jokes."

Maurice did not forget, however. He got laughs when he imitated others. He got more laughs as he developed his own style.

Tall and lean, no one realized the age or background of the naïve nineteen-year-old who became the opening act for performers appearing at such places as the Golden Cocktail Lounge at East 128th Street and Miles Avenue. He made more money from comedy than from music, opening for the Manhattans, the Ohio Players, the Dramatics, the Staple Singers, Gladys Knight and the Pips and others. Some of the material was Reedus's own creation; some he quoted from old Redd Foxx material he heard his father use. "I didn't know what some of the jokes meant," a sheepish Reedus admits.

> I'd tell the jokes, using the words and gestures my daddy used, and everyone would laugh. But I didn't know what I was saying. Like there was a joke where you never said the punch line, you just waited for them to get it. I might say, "What's the difference between a hard sleeper and a light sleeper? Well, a light sleeper sleeps with the light on." Then you leave the rest for them to think about. There's this quiet as they're thinking about it. It takes them a while to think about it, and then they're laughing.

The comedy routine was kept independent of the music in those early days with Foreign Blue. Instead of playing off one of the band members while out in the audience, as Reedus would do with Sly, Slick & Wicked, he would come back on stage after the other musicians took a break. He would take a stool, sit down and start to tell jokes for the next ten to fifteen minutes.

> I might start with something like, "You know how most entertainers come out and dedicate their show to all the pretty people in the audience? Well, I dedicate my show to all the ugly people. That way I have more friends." Then I'd pause and say, "Oh, yeah, you don't have to believe me but just look at the person next to you."

Then I might say, "You know, you really have to believe in Halloween. When I first met my old lady, I thought she had a mask on." I'd pause and say, "When I woke my wife up this morning, I said, Henry…" I'd wait until they realized it was the punch line, then look at them and say, "Well, you got your problems and I got mine."

Or I might say, "You got to see my old lady to believe in Halloween. She's ugly for no particular reason. She looks like Mike Tyson in a pink negligee.

"They said, would you take her for better or for worse. And I said, 'Hell, I think I'd like to take better. I can't do no worse.' I got to take her everywhere I go to keep from having to kiss her goodbye. She was so cross-eyed, when she cried, the tears ran down her back.

One day we were talking and I said, 'Baby, where you going?' And she said, 'I'm going downtown to buy me a brassiere.' And I said, 'For what? You ain't got shit to put in it.' She said, 'Hell, you wear shorts.'"

YOUNG MUSICIANS

Maurice and one of his first bands, a ten-piece group called the Metronome, which played regularly for clubs such as the Native Son on 153rd and Kinsman, experienced all the negative sides of being young musicians. They would go to the downstairs dressing room and there would be a man named Willy Cooper who provided cocaine to the musicians. Willy liked the shows and he liked the business he generated with the young players. During intermission, Willy would go downstairs where Maurice and several of the others lined up like a football team waiting to hear from their coach. They changed their clothes and then returned to the stage one at a time. A guitar player might go out and start playing, perhaps followed by a trumpet player, a drummer, a sax player and so forth. Each would pick up his instrument in turn, picking up the number wherever the other musicians had reached in the song.

Willy Cooper stood by the door leading from the dressing area to the stage. He would have a holder on which there were lines of cocaine equal to the number of musicians who were using it. Then he handed the first musician a straw through which he'd snort the drug, passing the straw to the next in line as he went out and started playing. They never had enough drugs to keep them from playing well, never enough to create addiction, though it was probably not from lack of desire. Willy gave the lines on credit, collecting his money at the end of the evening when the band members were paid. Willy was never certain how much the musicians would make for the evening so he limited his risk, inadvertently saving them from themselves.

Sometimes we had to play three shows a night, each with different songs. We'd change clothes for each show, and each time we went down to the dressing room, Willy would be there with the coke. Sometimes he'd give us the first lines for free, but then we'd have to pay for all the lines after that. The price was always the same, and we knew what we'd owe, but we never were sure of the house so some of the guys owed Willy for a past show. He knew we'd pay and he never pressured us.

No one ever knew what Willy was doing with the Metronome members. The musicians often had their girlfriends in the audience, and none of them knew either. The players would go downstairs tired at the end of a set and then come back up on stage refreshed. The audience just assumed they were rested from their breaks.

"Drug" of Choice

It was the comedy that became Maurice's "drug" of choice to stimulate his career.

Watching my daddy and Redd Foxx taught me to use little short bits and leave the audience hanging. Like they'd come on stage and say, "Good evening, ladies and gentlemen...and you others." You wouldn't explain. You'd let them think whatever they were going to think.

Sometimes it was like they didn't get it. It was a dead audience so I'd say, "I know this is good because I got it off the album and they laughed on the album." And then they'd laugh, but I still didn't know if they get it.

Maurice had hoped that the comedy would get him closer to the audience because he was shy and afraid to talk with people. Then he discovered that they were afraid to talk with him. Some thought a comedian was much smarter than they were, and they didn't know what to say. Others heard his material, and there was enough that would be classified as X-rated that they were afraid that if they tried to carry on a casual conversation with him, he would start saying things that would embarrass them. It was an awkward learning experience, but he was making more money than from his first love, playing the saxophone.

Sly, Slick & Wicked realized that Maurice enhanced their act with his comedy. Using physical props similar to those of his father, Maurice developed a way to segue into his comedy routine. The group would perform, and during the last number of their first set, Maurice would slip off stage, put on a farmer's coveralls and straw hat, take an extra long cigarette holder and a glass with whatever nonalcoholic mix looked like whiskey and sneak into the back of the audience. Then, when the number was over, Maurice would stand up and shout, "Boo! Boo, Boo, Boo!"

The audience would be shocked. No one recognized the man now pacing the back of the crowd as being the same one who had been playing the saxophone behind Sly, Slick & Wicked. Sometimes he moved from table to table, sitting down and complaining about the act. Other times he just roamed, heckling for a minute or two. And in one club, a police officer working off duty as a bouncer tried to arrest him before he realized the heckling was part of the act, a preliminary to Maurice going on stage to start the comedy.

Just before heading for the stage, Maurice would ask one of the musicians, "What's in back of the stage?"

"What do you mean, what's in back of the stage?" replied the musician, who was acting as straight man for the comedy.

"What's in back of the stage?" Maurice would repeat.

"Ain't nothing's in back of the stage," said the musician, clearly fed up with what the audience still thought was a heckler.

"I know," said Maurice. "Ain't nothing in front of it neither."

And then the laughter began as the audience gradually realized what was happening.

The musician on stage, seemingly tired of the taunting, told Maurice that if he thought he was so good, he should come up and entertain the audience himself. Then the musicians walked off the stage for the break while Maurice entertained the audience with his comedy routine.

Over time, young Reedus would develop his own material and his own style, imitating the pacing of both Redd Foxx and Maurice Reedus Sr. but evolving in ways that made him uncomfortable. He was unable to forget that he was made to believe he was stupid when he was growing up and going to school. He lived in fear that he would forget the material or not do something right. Those who knew him well also believe that there was a second fear, a fear he had yet to express. There was a chance that Maurice

Maurice Reedus Jr.: Sax in the City

Reedus Jr., perhaps because of his inability to read music, was evolving into a more innovative performer than his father, a man who traveled the world as a musician, played with the greats and periodically had a day job teaching college. The idea that his talent might be greater than his father's, that he might have greater success than the man he idolized, caused him to never let himself take the next step to success whenever it presented itself.

Reedus faced an additional challenge with the clubs he worked. Some clubs have a different crowd for each show. The first show, perhaps at 8:00 p.m., might have a younger audience or an audience of married couples who had to get home early because a sitter was watching their kids. There might be a two-drink minimum and/or a cover charge, but the audience was sober, attentive and wanting to laugh.

The second show would be about 10:00 p.m. Now you had a dating crowd with a number of them thinking about whether or not they would get lucky and have sex. The drinking was heavier, but the crowd was still relatively sober.

The third show typically would start at midnight or later. The audience would be drinking and would become foolish or belligerent, easily angered or easily bored, depending on how the alcohol was affecting them. It was an audience that enjoyed outrageous material that might have been offensive to the eight o'clock crowd.

The clubs where Reedus and the bands performed encouraged people to stay all evening—eating, drinking, talking and dancing. There would still be three shows, but in these clubs there would be the same audience. They might get increasingly drunk and belligerent. They might get increasingly mellow. But where the clubs that offered three separate shows allowed a comedian to use some of the same material in each show, in these all-evening clubs, Maurice had to have triple the material he might otherwise need.

The comedy was so good that when he was touring with his music, Maurice and a friend stopped in the famed Comedy Store in Los Angeles. It was an open-mike night where amateurs tried to gain experience in front of an audience and professionals tried out new material before using it on tour and on television.

Encouraged by a friend, Maurice stepped onto the stage and started talking. He told the jokes he had mastered, relaxed before an audience he knew he would never see again. And when he was done, he was the most popular performer that night. Some of the old professionals who had stopped by the club recognized that Maurice was using material in the manner of Redd Foxx, and they told him how impressed they were that he had brought back the style.

The Comedy Store made a practice of keeping a record of everyone who performed, and Maurice soon began getting calls to return. The club wanted him to perform for pay. There would be no more free gigs, and the exposure he would get made appearances in other clubs and on national television a certainty.

The recognition was unexpected. It was also overwhelming. Not only was Maurice insecure about his ability, but also such success would greatly overshadow what his father had accomplished with the comedy in his own act. The emotions were devastating. Maurice never returned the calls and never returned to the club. He did try other open-mike nights in other comedy clubs while in California, but he never had the courage to see how far he could go.

The young Reedus's insecurity as a stand-up was overcome with the help of John (Sly) Wilson who became Maurice's mentor and close friend. But Wilson never knew that Maurice could not read.

Reedus was certain he would be mocked at best and fired at worst, and he was finally doing work he loved, work he never wanted to leave. He asked John to go over the music with him, a request that was not unusual for someone who had to learn the timing and the way the three singers worked. And because Reedus could learn by observation and hearing the sounds, no one realized that he was the one professional musician in the group who had no idea what was written on the music pages they used.

SLY, SLICK & WICKED

While Reedus was gaining experience, Sly, Slick & Wicked were having the success that would eventually lead to their being named to both the Rock and Roll Hall of Fame and the Motown Hall of Fame. Before Reedus joined the group as a sax man, they recorded "Stay My Love," a song that led Paramount Records, a division of Paramount Motion Pictures, to sign them on March 22, 1971. Then, with major promotion behind the record, the song rose to number one on various charts.

Approximately two years later, in 1973, James Brown spotted Sly, Slick & Wicked, loved what he heard and signed them to his People (Polydor Records) label, making them a part of what he called his "First Family of Soul." When they wrote and recorded "Sho Nuff," produced by James Brown, the record was so successful that Don Cornelius signed the singers to appear on *Soul Train*, the longest-running and most widely seen music show in the world.

The three Cleveland singers moved on, becoming part of the O'Jays' Shaker Records and recording their next major hit, "Turn On Your Love Light," in 1974. It was a recording that brought them fame in Europe and Canada, not just the United States. Approximately two years later, Sly, Slick & Wicked was signed by Motown.

Maurice watched the changes with pride for his friends, but he did not realize that they were using him when they toured because of the quality of his music and his showmanship on stage. In his mind, he was still the kid with the bad grades, the class clown—a fraud because he could not read the music. He was being carried by the others, who, in his mind, apparently felt sorry for him. He never realized that they were touring with him because of the dimension he added to their shows. They were too professional to risk using someone who couldn't carry his own weight.

And then came the invitation to appear in the 1975 Kool Jazz Festival, at the newly opened Royals Stadium in Kansas City. Only the best acts in the nation were to appear—the legendary Count Basie Orchestra, Cannonball Adderly and B.B. King. Sly, Slick & Wicked had been chosen because of their success with James Brown and their exposure on *Soul Train*.

Maurice and the others arrived in Kansas City a couple of days before the festival, taking the time to rest, see the city and rehearse. Instead of the more familiar Motel 6, they were in a luxury hotel with all the food they ate in the restaurant or through room service provided free.

"We drove out to the stadium for a sound check," Maurice recalls. The stadium was empty, but people were standing around the area just outside the special parking area for celebrities. "I looked, and it was like a dream come true. I thought that everything would be uphill from there."

John Wilson remembers the moment a little differently. "Maurice looked up and whispered, 'This is big, Pete. This is really big. We're in the big time. I can't believe it.'"

They were taken to their dressing area, a large room that was divided by a sheet. Sly, Slick & Wicked, along with their backup band, were on one side; Count Basie was on the other. Maurice talked with Count Basie for a few minutes. The elderly musician knew his dad's work and encouraged Maurice to follow his own dreams wherever they led. "He told me to 'love music for the love of music and it will take you where you want to go.'"

The Count Basie Orchestra was the first act to go on stage. Maurice watched the performance, staring at the audience that had grown to eighty thousand fans. "There were people everywhere," he remembered, and he began to worry about how he would look, how he would sound. Sly had told them that they would be playing three songs—"Standing on Shaky Ground," "Turn on Your Love Light" and "Love Won't Let Me Wait." The last one startled Maurice when it was first announced. It had a sax solo.

When it was time for Sly, Slick & Wicked to go to the stage, two golf carts arrived at the dressing area, and all but Maurice got into the first cart. The crowd was a blur of color and sound; people were waving, and Maurice waved back. He looked cool. He felt terrified.

And then they were all on stage, playing the songs they had played in clubs holding at most three hundred or four hundred people. Maurice concentrated on the music, never thinking about where he was or what it meant. His friends were the professionals, not him. He was there. He was playing.

Then they were doing "Love Won't Let Me Wait," reaching the point where Sly, Slick & Wicked did their choreographed movements as Maurice put his horn to his lips and started blowing his solo.

Maurice Reedus Jr. *Photograph by Ted Schwarz.*

Maurice Reedus Jr.: Sax in the City

I looked up and there were these two big [video] screens. All I saw was my picture and then my fingers playing the sax. They had cameras out there and they were focused on me. I prayed my guardian angel was looking out for me and I wouldn't make any mistakes.

When it was over, he suddenly realized that eighty thousand people had risen to their feet and were cheering the group, cheering the soloist, acknowledging the brilliance of what they had just heard.

Too numb to register what was taking place, Maurice rode back to the dressing area to find Count Basie waiting for him. Sly, Slick & Wicked were the stars whose success had led them to be invited to Royals Stadium. Sly, Slick & Wicked were the names on the program. Sly, Slick & Wicked had put on the performance of their lives. But Count Basie and several members of his orchestra, men who had played with and listened to professionals throughout the world, walked over to Maurice. They more than anyone understood what had just happened—that a normally invisible musician officially backing the stars had magically transcended and, for the length of the solo, taken control of the stage.

Basie reached for Maurice's hand first, gripping it firmly in both of his own. "Young man," said Basie, "you did an excellent job. You knocked me out with the solo."

Maurice now recalls what may have been the happiest time of his life. "I thought there was no way we could go but up."

Success was not what Maurice thought it might be. There were women—there were always women—including a beautiful young nurse who met Maurice on the first night of a two-week series of shows in British Columbia. The two of them talked, learning about each other's work, their dreams and their values. The relationship was a deeply emotional one, as close to love at first sight as Maurice would ever come in his life.

By the end of the two weeks, Maurice and the nurse were engaged to be married. She would move to Cleveland, taking a job at one of the hospitals, accompanying him on the road when she could and waiting faithfully when only he was able to travel.

Weddings were women's work, men coming along for the ceremony. Call my mother, Maurice told his fiancée. The two of you can arrange everything. And then, following a passionate goodbye, Maurice continued touring with the group. What Maurice had not bothered to mention, leaving that chore to his long-suffering mother, was that he was already married. He never heard from the nurse again and had the good sense to not pursue her after he had his own inevitable divorce.

The hardest part of the road for Maurice was the reality of the payment as the group traveled among small towns and big cities. The pay was so low that they were often too broke for food, one time splitting sticks of gum among themselves. They had a manager. They traveled in an expensive car. But everyone stole from the band—club owners had them play before packed houses on the weekends and then return on Monday for their money only to discover the club locked and the owner "out of town." They had to travel to their next gig and were forced to leave their pay behind.

At other times, it was their manager who stole from them, keeping a percentage of the group's percentage of the box office. John Wilson—the "Sly" of Sly, Slick & Wicked—commented:

> *Getting paid, no matter how successful you were, could be tricky. You would get a small guarantee and a percentage of the take at the door. But that meant someone like our manager, Robert "Pete" Fulsom, would have to stand at the door with a clicker, count the heads, and make sure all that money added up. And sometimes, well, it's just like the Blues Brothers. You ate some food or the group, the band, drank some beers, and we're going to deduct it. If you made $500 that night, the manager would say you drank $450 worth of beer. Or you see the club is packed but he'll say he didn't have a full house. That was very common with the chittlin' circuit clubs.*

What was also common was access to women. However, there were rules that Fulsom maintained for the young musicians in his care.

Fulsom was an odd man, perhaps four hundred pounds and with a heart so stressed that his voice had a soft wheeze, a little like a bellows leaking air. Yet despite his size, he wore suits that were always cleaned and pressed, and his body was spotlessly clean. He was a man who could sweat without having any odor about him. And for reasons none of the musicians could understand, their manager always had at least one beautiful young woman on his arm and more often two. They were not using Fulsom to meet the seemingly more appropriate young musicians. They were focused solely on him, though no one understood why.

The women who were interested in the band members received a lecture from Folsom. He took them aside and told them that they had to feed the band at the very least. If they weren't willing to take one or more home, giving them a place to stay while in town, and to feed them, they should get out of the dressing room and away from the band's break area. The lecture was harsh, rude and presumptuous. It also worked, though sometimes too well. According to one of the musicians who occasionally toured with Maurice in that era:

> *There were places where you couldn't get penicillin if you were black and on the road. We used to try and get more than we needed, more than we hoped we'd need, and take it with us. Then, if we got into trouble in one of those cities where black people, especially black show business people, couldn't get medical help, we had our own supply to carry us until we found a doctor to treat whoever had the problem.*

Touring for Maurice was like being a part of a family whose home changed on a nightly basis. But the problems eventually outweighed the pleasures, especially when he realized that his joy was in performing. He wanted people to like him, like his work. That was why comedy made him happy. That was why he realized it did not matter to him where he played so long as he had an audience he could please.

The road still had its frustrations, like the club owners and managers seemingly forever trying to cheat him. He also knew from his conversations with his father and the older musicians his father played with that the problems were the same for every generation of traveling musicians, and the rewards always came from the performance. So long as someone wanted to hear Maurice, to focus their attention on the jokes he was telling or the music he was playing, he was a happy man. That was when he realized he got the same satisfaction from playing locally with one or another group and using styles ranging from reggae to soul to big band sounds. It was true that the money he earned was frequently less than he could earn on the road, but the chance of actually receiving it was greater, and he didn't have to drive so far to do it. And that was when Maurice Reedus Jr. mostly turned his back on national fame and whatever fortune it might have brought him, shifting his playing to the streets of Cleveland, disappearing in flamboyant dress and music more likely to reflect the theme songs of cartoons and reruns of old family-oriented comedies from the 1950s and 1960s than Duke Ellington or James Brown.

STREET MUSIC

It was in 1996 that the transformation occurred. Maurice and a friend had been at a rehearsal for one of the bands in which Maurice performed, and when they reached the bus stop at East Sixth and Prospect, they realized

This page: Maurice Reedus Jr.
Photograph by Ted Schwarz.

they didn't have enough money for the trip and to get something to eat. They were tired. They were hungry.

"I had my sax," he recalls,

> and this cat I was with said, "Take your horn out, brother, and start blowing your horn." I'd heard of street musicians, I just never thought about it. So I just took my horn out and started playing, and people started dropping money in there, and I started getting happy because I had my bus fare, too, and they kept dropping money and dropping money. Back then the first song that I played, it was "My Favorite Things." And then I started doing songs like the Addams Family [theme]. Songs I never played before but I just knew them from hearing them. So I just started playing all the songs that I grew up listening to.

Cleveland had a history of musicians playing in nontraditional areas, as well as in upscale hotel lobbies. Over the years, violinists played in front of the Old Arcade, defining their work as a street gig. Today, there are musicians who arrange to play for lunch hours inside such locations as the Old Arcade. But Maurice was probably the first truly committed for the long term, and he certainly is the most experienced professional Cleveland street musician, a choice he made because of his first successes.

> I wasn't panhandling. I'm a musician. I never got arrested, but I used to get hassled. Then [Mayor] Mike White used to tell me to keep up the good work. Then [Mayor] Jane Campbell said, "You're like an icon to the city. You keep doing what you're doing."

And Mayor Frank Jackson's staff arranged for Maurice to play in the rotunda of Cleveland City Hall surrounded by photographs of Reedus playing on the streets.

The sight and sound of Maurice Reedus Jr. was immortalized in a new way because of another serendipitous experience. He had been playing his saxophone outside Jacobs Field on an afternoon when the Indians were playing and crowds were streaming past, some people stopping to listen, some dropping money in the bucket he keeps near his sax case and some seemingly oblivious to his presence. Then a van pulled over and parked.

As with much of Maurice's life, opportunities just happen. Sometimes he has gone along with one; other times he has drifted away. This time, when several people came out of the van, he decided to say "yes" when they asked him if he wanted to be in a movie. He would not have to audition. He would be on their VIP list, and they would provide him with meals, the clothes he would need and two weeks of guaranteed paid work. And that was how, when Cleveland's Euclid Avenue was transformed into the streets of New York City, Maurice, who calls himself "Cleveland's Sax Man," was turned into a Manhattan street musician and appeared in the movie *Spiderman 3*.

The movie did not jump-start a new career for Maurice. Instead, a number of factors came together to give him yet another opportunity he remains reluctant to consider since it would take him to Florida. That would involve working for a musician who has known him since the days of touring with Sly, Slick & Wicked. However, the death by cancer of both his parents came as a shock to Reedus, one from which he has yet to fully recover. He still finds himself thinking of his father or playing a recording of his music late at night and then crying himself to sleep.

At the same time, he has begun returning to more serious performing, still on the street but with one or more other musicians who will not let him play less than his best.

The first warm day of spring, for example, found Maurice and a professional guitar player/songwriter/recording studio owner named Ghani standing in the center of Public Square, putting on a concert for no reason other than the sun was shining, the birds were singing and people were delighted to be outside during their lunch hour. In previous months, Reedus seemed only to worry about pleasing passersby and constantly shifted from the opening of one song to the opening of another, a habit that diminished his reputation. ("I just want to make people happy," he replied when asked why he didn't play a number all the way through. "He's just lazy," commented a fellow musician whose blues band plays more traditional venues in the Cleveland area.) That day, "controlled" by Ghani who insisted they play serious music all the way through, regardless of the response, Maurice discovered how much his frequently hidden talents were appreciated. He not only played songs in their entirety, but he also caressed the notes like a lover and then improvised the music, sometimes the sound wailing with joy, other times dancing about the ears of the listeners. It was a virtuoso performance for both Ghani and Maurice, and the lunch crowd understood that they were hearing something special.

Soon, men with suits were dancing with well-dressed women they had never encountered until that moment. Some swayed in front of the two musicians like a date crowd in a 1940s-era nightclub clustered around the big band performing on the stage. Others moved about the sidewalk, eyes closed, dancing with a partner of the imagination.

Maurice Reedus Jr.: Sax in the City

Maurice Reedus Jr. *Photograph by Ted Schwarz.*

And Maurice Reedus Jr., normally a shy, insecure man of enormous talent, did something he rarely did when he played on the streets. He lowered his sax while Ghani soloed and then looked at the crowd all about him. He saw the dancers. He saw the occasional singer whose karaoke experience caused him to be unable to hold back the lyrics, though sung quietly so as not to break the mood the two professionals had created. And then he put the mouthpiece to his lips and once again wailed with joy.

Maurice Reedus Jr. is the only featured Clevelander still living. He is arguably the best known, at least by sound and by sight. Since in recent years he has been the city's only full-time "busker," it seemed that no book on the unusual characters of the city would be complete without including him. In addition, Reedus has been offered a chance to join a successful band based in Florida; he has also had an offer from a documentary film company to come to the city to record his life. Yet he remains insecure about his talent and uncertain what he needs to do to get the public to like him when he performs. The Maurice Reedus Jr. everyone recognizes on the downtown streets is also the top musician nobody really knows.

Fast Eddie Watkins

On May 16, 1980, a letter was mailed to WKYC television news anchors Doug Adair and Mona Scott. "I thought I'd drop a fast hello to my favorite TV station. The cops didn't think I'd have the nerve to visit their city. Just wanted them to know I like Cleveland." Then the letter writer entered Central National Bank at 3279 West 117th Street and announced, "I'm Eddie Watkins, the famed bank robber."

Eddie was right. Fifteen years earlier, in 1965, he reached the high point in his career notoriety, a fact that always pleased him. He robbed five Cleveland-area banks and a sixth in Columbus, a feat that enabled him to attain the honor role of bad guys—the FBI's Ten Most Wanted list.

Eddie Watkins fancied himself the "last of the big-time bank robbers," though the truth was that he seemed to prefer getting his name in the newspapers to getting away clean with the money he stole. He not only introduced himself to tellers and management, but he also created in his mind the equivalent of a Michelin guide to vulnerable banks. The guide, a rating system he memorized and happily shared, gave banks from one star (most difficult to rob) to five stars (easiest to stickup).

There was Central National Bank at 3279 West 117th, for example. Eddie had cased the bank in October 1975 and was so pleased with what he found (five stars) that he was heading there to rob the tellers on October 30 of that year. The only problem, as with so many of Eddie's actions when not in jail, was that he got arrested in Society National Bank, at 13681 Lorain Avenue (rating unknown), which he was trying to rob before moving on to his primary target—Central National.

The five-star Central National Bank was like one's first love—it may end badly, but you can never forget what you meant together. As his wife was

Right: Fast Eddie Watkins, October 31, 1975, at age fifty-six. *Courtesy of Cleveland State University's Cleveland Press Collection.*

Below: Fast Eddie Watkins, August 16, 1966. *Courtesy of Cleveland State University's Cleveland Press Collection.*

quoted as saying, "Most men ogle girls. Eddie ogles banks." Eddie's arrest was robbery interruptus, and Central National was like the beautiful mistress who had just started removing her clothes so her lover could share her most intimate places when he was suddenly pulled away from her bed.

For almost five years, while Eddie was serving time in the federal penitentiary in Atlanta, he thought of returning to Central National Bank. Week after week and month after month, Eddie sought ways to escape his prison and return to Cleveland. Finally, on April 29, 1980, well before his sentence was up, he fled his confinement and went in pursuit of the five-star bank that had gotten away.

The prison escape had been relatively simple. He had managed to steal an orange prison pickup truck whose appearance was so outlandish that the guards apparently could not imagine that a prisoner would use it instead of trying to remain inconspicuous.

Eddie took a circuitous way back to Cleveland. On May 8, he was in Los Angeles where he went to a used car dealership and talked with a salesman about buying a car. The two men climbed into the one that Eddie said interested him and then Eddie drove until he was close to a branch of Citizens Savings & Loan. He forced the salesman from the car, drove to the bank, went inside and left with $606, more than enough to pay for the $286 one-way flight to Cleveland.

Finally, Eddie was reunited with his lost love, the same Central National Bank branch he had planned to rob five years earlier. To his delight, the institution remained a five-star facility. There would be plenty of money.

There was more to this rendezvous than the FBI realized, though they had been certain he would return to Cleveland after he escaped Atlanta. Eddie needed recognition for his achievements. He wore a hat because he always wore a hat. However, he kept it at an angle that would reveal his face because he wanted to be known for his accomplishment. Then, in case the security cameras did not get a clear picture of him, he planned to announce his presence.

It was 1:40 p.m. when Eddie first entered the bank. He asked to see the manager, Ronald Dietrich, but the man had stepped out for a while. Eddie said he would be back. No one else could help him.

Thirty minutes later, with Dietrich now at his desk, Eddie reentered the bank, walked to the manager's desk and sat down in the chair opposite. Then he reportedly said, "I am Eddie Watkins. I'm the famed bank robber. I'm going to rob this bank."

No weapon was visible, though Eddie was carrying what appeared to be a lunch bag in which witnesses said there was definitely a handgun. "Do what I say. Don't move your hands or make any sudden moves or I'll blow your f------ head off." The language may have been foul, but it was not spoken loudly. Watkins was gentle and polite, and though he wanted credit for his actions, he had no intention of causing undue concern.

There were a half dozen customers in the bank, but Eddie had no interest in them. Instead, he and Dietrich walked from teller station to teller station, asking each employee to empty the contents of the cash drawer into a second bag Eddie was carrying. Then he walked out the rear door as a teller called police.

CRIMINAL CAREER

Eddie robbed banks, but he also saw them as the safest repository for the more than $1.5 million he stole in his forty-three-year career involving more than fifty-five banks from Cleveland to Los Angeles. "I trust banks with my money—they're insured. It's the best place in the world to put your money."

Watkins, who had already spent thirty-nine years behind bars when he made his Atlanta escape, began his lifetime career in 1935, when he was sixteen and robbed his first bank, netting $2,400. Two years later, not yet recognizing what would become his lifelong specialty, he worked with a partner who may or may not have been a willing companion—his cousin, Dorothy Zecchini, age twenty-five, the married mother of two children.

Zecchini, who later claimed to be a victim of Eddie's threats, seemed to enjoy her life on the wild side when she was known as the "giggling girl" robber, and Watkins had yet to make the frequent, successful escapes from banks and prisons that gave him his nickname of "Fast Eddie." However, she was first quoted as considering herself a victim in what the police thought was a self-serving statement. Describing her first night of crime late in October 1937, she said:

> *On Hough Avenue, Watkins* [who was driving] *drew to the curb, hopped out and tried to snatch a woman's purse. Then he drove me home. He threatened to shoot me and my husband if I told on him.*
>
> *Saturday night he drove me to the grocery store. When we got in front of it he said he was going to rob the place. I told him not to. We argued and fought and he drove around the block ten times.*
>
> *Then he said he would tell the police I was with him in the purse snatching and have me locked up if I didn't do what he said. He wrote a note and I took it in and handed it to the clerk in the store. Watkins stood with a gun* [later identified as a .22-caliber target pistol] *and took the money. I went out with him.*

Dorothy's stories of her crime spree with Watkins included bakeries, gasoline stations and other businesses, carefully chosen but without the sense of specialization he developed later when he focused solely on banks. Dorothy herself had a tendency to giggle during the robberies. The giggle may have been because she was enjoying herself or it may have been out of nervousness. Whatever the case, the press named her the "giggling girl" robber, and she sometimes signed the notes passed demanding money "Giggling Girl." Later, she claimed that Eddie's sixteen-year-old girlfriend must have been the giggling girl during one night's sprees when the teenager took her place. However, that was later proven false.

Perhaps the most outrageous moment in Watkins's career as bank robber, escape artist and self-promoter came on June 7, 1980, when a desperate Edward Watkins could not outrun a trap set by the police and FBI. At 10:00 a.m. that morning, when Eddie had been hiding in a Euclid, Ohio apartment, someone who knew him called in a tip. The caller said that Eddie was driving south on Interstate 71 in a Mercury Cougar. An hour and a half later, having been spotted, seven police cars and an unknown number of federal agents were engaged in a slow-speed chase while Eddie left the freeway and turned north on Ohio 83. Agents had positioned themselves on White Road, and when Eddie slowed to turn right, the agents shot out his tires.

Watkins had vowed never to be taken alive, never to go back to prison. And that morning, in a desperate effort to protect himself from arrest by the overwhelming force confronting him, he grabbed a hostage. Then, placing a gun to the hostage's head, he warned the police to stay away.

There was only one problem with the action that proved to be as outrageous as the rest of Watkins's career. He held the gun to the head of the only person present who wasn't in law enforcement—himself. Eddie was once again returned to jail.

"I WANTED TO BE A BIG SHOT"

It's probably an ego thing, but I never really thought about doing anything else.
Everybody has got to have something to be proud of.
—Eddie Watkins

There would be other crimes, including a bank robbery during which nine hostages were held for twenty-one hours, the only situation in his long career that he seemed to regret. Still, no one was physically harmed, a fact that pleased Eddie.

Fast Eddie Watkins

On March 18, 2002, Eddie was in Cleveland for the last time. He was eighty-two years old and suffering from heart and lung disease when he entered the hospital. His death ended a forty-three-year criminal career that, during those times he was back on the streets, enabled him to achieve his goals. As he explained to a reporter for the *Plain Dealer*: "I wanted to be a big shot. I wanted to buy fancy cars. I wanted to impress the women. I wanted to have a pocket full of money when I walked into that casino in Las Vegas." And briefly, Fast Eddie had it all.

Effa Manley's Secret Cleveland Visit

The story of baseball great Larry Doby's coming to Cleveland to play for the Indians has been told many times and in many ways. It was the summer of 1947. Bill Veeck, a one-legged promotion genius, celebrated all victories and occasionally what others might consider defeat, such as when he rented the Hollenden Hotel ballroom to throw a coming out party for his newly arrived wooden leg. He danced every dance, the stress breaking the wood and forcing him to crawl back to the table, regretting he hadn't ordered a spare.

Over the years, he held such events as Ethnic Nights (when he owned the Chicago team), celebrating such groups as the local Croatians. He added additional sports to the baseball experience, such as beer-case stacking. He claimed that this was the traditional sport of any number of immigrants, including the Irish, Polish and Germans, defying anyone to claim otherwise. During a variety of music nights, there were promotions such as half-price tickets for anyone entering with an instrument. (No instrument? You were handed a kazoo to present at the box office as proof that you deserved to pay only half.) And then, when he had utilized every variation he could imagine, including having Chicago Symphony Orchestra associate conductor Henry Mazer in the white tie and tails routinely used during formal concerts lead the "orchestra" of more than eighty thousand instrument-toting fans in a seventh-inning-stretch rendition of "Take Me Out to the Ballgame," he had a promotion that involved exploding thousands of record albums containing disco music.

With all the outrageous actions, the one side of Bill Veeck that was overlooked was his passion for fairness. Perhaps it was the fact that he was crippled. (He hated the term "disabled," seeing it as unrealistic for defining life with one useable leg. Had he lived, he would have vilified anyone daring to speak of him as being "differently abled.") Perhaps he simply was a truly honorable man who hid his heart from the public until he had to stand up for another.

For example, shortly after buying the Cleveland Indians, Veeck, who had been staying in the Hotel Cleveland (now the Renaissance), moved into a private club, never thinking about what it meant. The club had rooms that members could reserve for friends who were visiting Cleveland. This was all run much like a hotel, and to add to the exclusivity, the hotel proudly claimed to be "restrictive."

Cleveland, like many cities around the country, had a secret code of bigotry. Events promoted in the three daily newspapers—the *Plain Dealer*, the *News* and the *Press*—were open to white people only. It did not matter what the event might be. It did not matter where the event was held. The papers carried information for whites.

The *Call & Post* was the newspaper alerting "Negroes" to events in the city at which either everyone or black people were welcome. An event listed in the three major dailies *and* the *Call & Post* was open to anyone in the city with the possible exception of members of one or more religions and ethnic groups. A business that declared itself "restricted" was politely saying that anyone who was Jewish need not apply. This proved true with the club where Veeck was living when he went to reserve a room for a friend, Harry Grabiner, who was traveling regularly between his home in Michigan and Cleveland, where he was in business. The moment Veeck was told by the room clerk that Grabiner, being Jewish, could not stay in the club where Veeck was living, despite the guest suites being available, Veeck told the clerk he was leaving. He hurriedly packed and never again stayed in a "restricted" residence.

Veeck also studied the history of minority group advances in the United States, noting that blacks advanced through the courts. There was still extensive bigotry—as Veeck well knew, being the owner of a team that, at the time of purchase, was part of a profession that never allowed black players. However, in addition to the personal stand he was about to take that would greatly impact Cleveland, he also seriously considered studying for the law when he was in one of several "retirements." The immediate post–World War II years formed an era when many states still allowed the old practice of studying for the bar exam rather than going to college. A man had the option of reading law books and essentially teaching himself the law. Most did their reading in the firm of a willing mentor, ensuring that questions could be answered by a working professional and also ensuring a job after passing the exam.

Veeck planned to study the law as it affected Indians, both on reservations and in the cities. He thought he could improve their lives in the same way

Larry Doby, 1953. *Courtesy of Cleveland Public Library Photograph Collection.*

that men such as then attorney (later Supreme Court justice) Thurgood Marshall had done through the National Association for the Advancement of Colored People (NAACP). While Veeck never did become a lawyer, he did act in a manner that helped change a portion of society. He brought baseball player Larry Doby to Cleveland to play for the Indians.

Years later, Veeck wrote how he viewed the pursuit of Doby in a story still somewhat familiar to baseball fans. However, the action paled in comparison with the lesser-known decisions of Effa Manley, a woman who spent almost no time in Cleveland yet whose courage in relation to Doby transcended all but the great ballplayer himself.

As Veeck wrote in his memoirs (*Veeck as in Wreck*):

> *At the start of the 1947 season, I hired a Negro public relations man, Lou Jones, so that he could familiarize himself with the league ahead of time and serve as a companion and a buffer to the player we signed. I spoke to the leaders of the city and told them I was going to hold them responsible for policing their own people in case of trouble. (There was nothing for them to be responsible for, of course. We never had one fight in Cleveland in which a Negro was involved.)*

Effa Manley's Secret Cleveland Visit

I moved slowly and carefully, perhaps even timidly. It is usually overlooked, but if Jackie Robinson was the ideal man to break the color line, Brooklyn was also the ideal place. I wasn't that sure about Cleveland. Being unsure, I wanted to narrow the target areas as much as possible; I wanted to force the critics to make their attacks on the basis of pure prejudice—if they dared—and not on other grounds. To give them no opportunity to accuse us of signing a Negro as a publicity gimmick, I had informed the scouts that I wasn't necessarily looking for the best player in the Negro leagues but for a young player with the best long-term potential. And I only wanted to sign one Negro because, despite those glowing credentials I had given myself, I felt that I had to be in a position to extricate the club fairly easily in case we ran into too many problems.

(A humorous aside: Veeck wanted the Newark Negro League team—the Newark Eagles, on which Doby played—scouted the same way a white team would be looked at when an owner was seeking to add or change players. He also wanted the scouting done in secret. Toward that end, Bill Killifer, the scout chosen to make the evaluation, was sent to Newark over a weekend when the Eagles were playing. Newark also had a traditional white team playing in the International League, and Killifer, told nothing about Doby, assumed he was to scout those players. He also discovered that the International League game was out of town the weekend he arrived, and assuming there was a mistake, he ignored the Negro League game, went to a bar and got drunk. It was another two days before Killifer learned he was to look at the Newark Eagles. He found the next game and handled the scouting in a traditional manner.)

The timing for integrating baseball was not a publicity stunt. Veeck had long been interested in ending the segregation of the sport. However, he felt that by waiting until World War II was over and Americans of all races recognized the courage and achievements of the black soldiers, there would be a greater chance of acceptance.

Larry Doby was the brilliant second baseman of the Newark Eagles, and he rightly has been lauded for his courage in enduring the taunts of fans and fellow players when he came to Cleveland. His story has been told and retold over the years. The person who has mostly disappeared from the city's history is the woman who owned the Newark Eagles, Effa Manley.

There was probably no one connected with baseball who was more sensitive to the plight of the gifted black athlete or blacks in general than Manley. She was a white woman who passed as black, enduring the limitations, isolation and poor treatment afforded to her players. She could stay in any hotel she desired, but if a hotel denied a room to one of her players based on the color of his skin, she went

Larry Doby. *Courtesy of Cleveland Public Library Photograph Collection.*

to whatever hotel accepted him, "passing" as a light-skinned Negro.

Both Manley's parents were white, but the marriage ended, and her white mother married a black man who became Effa's stepfather, siring children who were half white and half black. She knew how her family was often shunned by both blacks and whites, though her half siblings were mostly able to go anywhere their father went.

Effa moved from Philadelphia, where, in 1900, she was born and raised, to New York, where she got a job in the millinery industry immediately after high school. She also fell in love with baseball, becoming a regular at the games, including the 1932 World Series when it was played at Yankee Stadium.

It was at the World Series that Effa met Abe Manley, a wealthy baseball fan whose money came from two sources. One was from real estate, a field he understood well enough to thrive during the Great Depression. The other business was what was politely called "numbers banking" if you had not been arrested and "racketeering" if you had done meaningful jail time. Abe, twenty-four years older than Effa, was in "numbers banking."

The Manleys, who married on June 15, 1935, decided that they should start their own baseball team in order to give skilled black players a place to show their accomplishments, which often were greater than those of the stars on the white teams. They formed their first team, the Brooklyn Eagles, named for the Brooklyn newspaper, and played in Ebbets Field before a limited number of fans. Their competition was the Brooklyn Dodgers, who used the same playing field and attracted a much larger crowd.

The answer for the Manleys was to move their team to Newark, buying the semipro black team called the Newark Dodgers and forming the Newark Eagles in 1936.

Effa Manley's Secret Cleveland Visit

Effa had been a social activist before becoming a businesswoman. She had joined the Citizen's League for Fair Play, and the year before she married Abe, she had helped organize a boycott of Harlem stores that refused to hire black salesclerks. The stores had been popular and their merchandise in demand, but Effa and others ensured that, after six weeks, the owners had to either start hiring fairly or go out of business. The impact was so great that a year later, the three hundred stores on 125th Street employed blacks.

Once resettled in Newark, Effa became the treasurer for the Newark chapter of the NAACP, often shocking people by the way she forced them to confront national social problems. For example, in 1939, the Newark Eagles baseball team had an "Anti-Lynching Day" in Ruppert Stadium, where they played.

Baseball was a seasonal sport, and the Manleys were concerned about professional ballplayers having to find second jobs for when the season was over. They went to Puerto Rico and started a winter league that would employ all the players who wanted to earn their living year-round in baseball. They also involved themselves in their players' personal lives, from making loans to showing up in church to act as the godparents of a baseball player's baby.

It was the Manleys who were instrumental in establishing the Negro Leagues, a business little understood by outsiders. There was a hunger for baseball among all Americans, but teams such as the Cleveland Indians denied blacks the opportunity to sit in the stands or to have a future as professional players. The Negro Leagues attracted both blacks and whites, and during World War II, when there were few forms of entertainment available, the games were a popular respite from war work. The Negro Leagues, one of the largest black-dominated businesses in 1945, was worth $2 million, far more than most white-owned corporations. And among the biggest beneficiaries was Effa Manley.

It is not known how long the Negro Leagues could have continued had there not been a major effort to integrate baseball, not just by the white owners such as Veeck, but also by Manley. She cared more about the young men who worked for her than her own growing wealth. Still, as she later wrote in her autobiography, she was caught off guard when, in the early summer of 1947, Abe told her that Bill Veeck was going to call.

"He didn't waste any time in coming straight to the point," Manley later wrote. "'Mrs. Manley, I want to make a deal for your Larry Doby. What is the price you want?'"

Manley explained that she would never stand in the way of Larry Doby if he wanted to play for the Indians:

Cleveland Indians owner Bill Veeck, who integrated baseball with Effa Manley of the Newark Eagles. *Courtesy of Cleveland Public Library Photograph Collection.*

"A scout of mine, Bill Kellefer, has been watching Doby for some time. We've come to the conclusion that he's about ready for the Big Leagues. I'll give you $10,000 for him."

I couldn't resist coming back with this rejoinder: "Mr. Veeck, you know if Larry Doby were white and a free agent, you'd give him $100,000 to sign with you merely as a bonus." There was a momentary pause. "However, I realize I'm in no position to be bargaining with you. If you feel you're being fair by offering us $10,000, I suppose we should accept."

Evidently I had scored a minor victory of sorts by injecting the racial injustice angle into our discussion.

"Mrs. Manley," Veeck continued, "I'll do this much in your case; If we keep Doby 30 days from the time we sign him up, I'll send you an additional five grand, which will make the total come to $15,000."

"In any event," I replied, "I must tell you my husband and I are full partners in this business. I'll have to get his approval. He's in Washington, where our team is playing. I'll have to call him first before I can give you any commitment."

Effa Manley knew what the business deal would mean on a personal basis, and Abe reinforced the problem when Effa reached him in Washington.

Larry Doby coming to Cleveland would wreck the Newark Eagles. The other players would be hurt if they learned Doby had been sold, and Doby would be hurt if he thought the club owners cared more about their team than about his future. The money, between $100,000 and $150,000 in today's dollars, was extremely low for a white player of Doby's skills.

Finally, both Manleys agreed that having Larry Doby go to Cleveland was in the best interest of both the athlete and black players in general. The only caveat had to do with money—Larry Doby's, not the Manleys':

> *We're paying Doby $4,000 a season right now. If he goes with you, I want you to assure me that he won't get less than $5,000 a year. I don't want this youngster kicked around.*
>
> *It was my understanding at the time that the few black players who had been signed by the Brooklyn Dodger organization (the ONLY club in the majors which had shown—up 'til then—the slightest interest in adding blacks to its playing roster) were being paid very little in the way of salaries.*

Manley later explained:

> *My information was that these players—with the possible exception of Jackie Robinson—all were averaging about $200–$300 a month apiece. I certainly didn't want Larry Doby to have to travel this kind of a route, not with all the great talent I knew he possessed.*

Veeck gave his word that Larry Doby would never play for less than $5,000 a year. He also made certain that Doby went from Newark to the Indians without having to spend any time in Cleveland's minor-league team.

Manley, self-effacing, never wrote the full story of Larry Doby's coming to Cleveland. Her book, *Negro Baseball...Before Integration*, only mentions July 5, 1947, when Larry Doby joined the Indians for the first time. The game was in Chicago's Comiskey Park, and the players gathered in the clubhouse to meet with manager Lou Boudreau, who was introducing the newest player. Doby later was quoted as saying:

> *All the players were standing around their lockers as I was introduced, one by one. I remember two of the players (who shall be nameless) refused to shake my hand. One was a regular on the team. But I'll never, never forget Joe Gordon, the Cleveland second baseman. He grabbed my hand and squeezed it hard. I felt much better after that.*

There was more. Larry Doby had to live with a hostile team and an even more hostile group of fans. But what has long gone unmentioned was the day, a few days after the Chicago games, when Doby played his first game in Cleveland. One of the fans in the stand, a woman who had to borrow a hotel room from a black friend so she could avoid having to take advantage of being white, was Effa Manley.

Perhaps more than her husband, Effa understood exactly what she had done by giving Larry Doby a chance to show his talent by playing for the largest audience in baseball. The Newark Eagles were favored to win the Negro League championship when their statistics were studied on July 4 (twenty-seven wins and fourteen losses). Without Doby, the team deteriorated just enough so that, on September 19, they were passed by their toughest rival, the New York Cubans. The difference was Doby.

Effa also knew that box office attendance would go down, and in those days the money came from the box office. Doby was the man who had produced the runs for the team. Doby was the draw that brought fifty thousand or more fans to the Negro League games. By 1948, with Doby solidly involved with Cleveland baseball and grudgingly being accepted, the Newark Eagles were doing well to play before just thirty-five thousand fans. The end of the season, with the Eagles placing third, was also the last time the team would play. That day in Cleveland, when Effa Manley cheered the success of Larry Doby and watched how he handled himself with dignity, despite the taunts of a type Effa had witnessed used against her stepfather and half siblings in their lives, was more dramatic than any sports writer or fan could know. Effa was watching the start of her deliberate destruction of the Negro Leagues. She had fought racism in baseball the only way she could—by destroying her franchise. With Larry Doby going to Cleveland, she ensured that in the near future, all baseball players, regardless of race or ethnic origin, would be judged and hired to play based solely on their skills as athletes.

And so Effa Manley became one of the most important Clevelanders, despite being in the city for just a day or two. She stood and watched. She cheered, even though Doby was still several games from being calm and comfortable enough to prove his brilliance. She cheered, though what was happening meant the loss of a multimillion-dollar business. She cheered, though in anonymity; Clevelanders only remembered Bill Veeck's giving a unique opportunity to Larry Doby and not the woman who came to the city to sacrifice her personal success so that others could prosper.

Laura Corrigan

Nobody in Cleveland liked Laura Corrigan; at least, nobody who mattered.

One problem was that the woman arrived in 1917, a time when the often-ruthless exploiters who had made their wealth in oil, steel, railroads, construction and retail, among other industries, were retiring or had passed on. These were the men honored as civic leaders instead of being sent to jail because they were one step ahead of the legislators and the courts. When there were public outcries demanding everything from anti-trust legislation to rules about workplace health and safety, the focus was on the action of the no longer active first generation of entrepreneurs. Their children, often the inheritors of great wealth and the "& Son" position in their fathers' corporations, were insulated from criticism by time and the acceptance of the new regulations for business and industry.

The wives of the men who formed the new generation of capitalists in Cleveland (and other large cities, for that matter) focused on the creation of a proper society. Some with access to almost obscene sums of money from their and their husbands' inheritances ran foundations and engaged in other good works, though frequently making certain they were regularly honored for what they did. Wings of hospitals, school buildings and fundraising events often had the donors' names attached, an honor they humbly accepted, never admitting that, without it, they might have shared their wealth with some other charity.

Some divided their time among two or more homes, each with a staff of servants to handle maintenance of the grounds, the mansion, the meals and the children and to act as chauffeurs for the family. They were executives of their estates, often using their homes for elaborate parties meant to impress others in similar circumstances.

And some maintained a lifestyle supportive of a husband who spent a portion of each day sitting in his stockbroker's office, checking the fluctuations of his wealth. Then there would be lunch at his in-town club, perhaps followed by golf at the country club (weather permitting) and then dressing for dinner at the same facility. The week was filled with activities at once self-indulgent, insular and defining what they considered proper behavior.

Children did happen in such a setting, and when they had been properly raised by nurses, nannies, finishing schools and colleges—whose degrees for women were often unrelated to any work the female graduates might consider in the world at large—an appropriate marriage was expected. This meant that a young man's choice, often carefully, albeit subtly, orchestrated by his elders, had to face one of the standard, unspoken tests of Cleveland society women.

A woman who was from a local family and had grown up attending the right schools, the right parties and the right balls would simply slip into the social scene as a junior member of whatever organization was in favor at the moment. A young woman from New York, Boston, Providence or some other city with its own carefully cultivated social register, no matter how prominent her family might be in that location, had to pass the grand dame test. The oldest, most respected leader of Cleveland's first families would look closely at the young upstart's face; the "proper" young lady would reflect back the older woman's visage as she had been when young and was just starting to be a part of the elite social circle.

Men raised in Cleveland society instinctively understood the game their mothers, wives and daughters played among themselves. Marriages were not arranged, but the circumstances leading to marriages could be. That was why Harvard was popular among the wealthy. It was quite common for a young man to graduate after placing an engagement ring on his college roommate's sister and taking a job in his soon-to-be father-in-law's business. This was true not only in Cleveland but also throughout the Midwest and along the East Coast. Harvard and a handful of other prestigious schools were known at the time less for their academic superiority than for the contacts that could be made during the four years in attendance.

Laura Mae Whitlock was from a far different background, one that did not include prestigious schools and society marriages. Her enemies considered her a social climber—a woman who would do whatever it took to gain a husband with status. Her friends considered her an independent woman who would pursue a man for love, not money or status. Whatever the case, Laura's life before coming to Ohio was as foreign to Cleveland's society leaders as theirs was to hers.

Little is known for certain about Laura's childhood, other than that she was born and raised in Stephens Point, Wisconsin. Her father was either a gardener or a lumberjack, maybe both or maybe something else, though definitely a laborer.

Laura's education is also unknown, though as a young woman seeking her fortune in the world, she traveled to Chicago, where she worked for a hotel. Some reports say she was a waitress in the hotel dining room. Others say she was the switchboard operator. No one accused her of improper behavior,

Laura Corrigan. *Courtesy of Cleveland State University's Cleveland Press Collection.*

just a lack of an appropriate pedigree to move to a higher station in life. As with all aspects of Laura's early years, no one thought the details were important; what mattered was that, in the minds of the social elite, she was never "one of us."

Duncan R. McMartin, MD, was the doctor for the hotel where Laura worked. He was available to assist guests who became injured, took ill or developed complications from chronic conditions. He would conduct an examination, write a prescription, send the guest to the hospital or let the guest know that there was no cause for immediate concern and he or she could enjoy his or her stay in Chicago, waiting until returning home for any treatment. He was on call twenty-four hours a day, a service seldom needed but appreciated by the guests. He was also either an alcoholic, a drug abuser or an incompetent—details not mentioned in the hotel's advertising.

Cleveland society leaders might hear that a woman has married a hotel doctor and consider her fortunate to achieve such a status as the wife of an MD is afforded. Chicago society leaders knew that hotels were the last medical employers of the incompetent and disreputable. It is likely that Laura met Dr. McMartin during times of sobriety, was courted when the doctor was at his best and then discovered why he was working in the hotel only after they were married and she could experience the man's unexpected failings in the course of an average week. Love was blind. It was also unable to change the self-destructive behavior of the lowest-status member of the medical profession.

CAPTAIN JAMES CORRIGAN

Captain James Corrigan was a first-generation Cleveland businessman whose money came from hard work in the steel industry. He partnered with longtime friend Price McKinney in creating the Corrigan-McKinney Steel Company, a business that would eventually be better known as Republic Steel Corporation. He also had financial deals with Frank Rockefeller, the lesser-known brother of Standard Oil's John D. Rockefeller. Given the growing demand for steel as the automobile came to dominate the roads, airplanes were being built for both the military and civilian flyers and high-rise construction was on the increase, it was no wonder that he became a multimillionaire.

The four-hundred-acre Corrigan estate, Nagirroc (Corrigan spelled backwards), was located in Wickliffe, a suburb of Cleveland. Captain

Corrigan also owned a yacht, the *Idler*, supposedly the grandest boat of its type on the Great Lakes. Such a yacht was a major status symbol among the wealthy, but James Corrigan would discover that it could also be the coffin of everything that truly mattered.

Lake Erie was the shallowest of the Great Lakes, a fact often lost on the captains of yachts and other vessels plying the normally placid water between Cleveland and Canada, from Michigan to Pennsylvania. Storms arise so quickly and so violently that a boat perhaps fifty feet from docking can be tossed about for an hour or more before it can move forward enough to throw a line to the dock.

On July 8, 1900, Ida Corrigan, James's wife; their three daughters; their infant granddaughter; and James's sister-in-law, Mary, were on board their luxury yacht being towed by the steamship *Australia* from Port Huron to Cleveland, a thirty-five-mile trip, when the sun became unusually bright. The family went below deck to be more comfortable.

On any of the other Great Lakes, the weather conditions of that July day would not have been a problem. A storm began moving toward Cleveland, the clouds moving swiftly, the water starting to roil, the winds slamming into the sails at sixty miles an hour and the boat rocking and in danger of capsizing. The crew members were wearing life jackets as they moved quickly about the deck, trying to cut the line connecting the *Idler* with the *Australia* and to lower or otherwise bring down the sails to keep the vessel upright. Nothing worked though, and the men were exhausted, clinging to the outside of the vessel when the rescuers came.

Inside the cabin, the Corrigans were being thrown about as the space began filling with water. The vessel was capsizing, and though an emergency call had gone out and was received by two nearby fishing tugboats, it would be twenty minutes before they arrived. By then, only the lifeguard-clad crew members clinging to the deck, and Mary Corrigan in the cabin, where she was clutching a cork-filled couch, were still alive.

The deaths of James Corrigan's family were emotionally overwhelming. He had loved his wife and loved the pleasures of children and family. To have them all dead in an instant on a waterway they had all once enjoyed was overwhelming. Yet once the shock eased, friends noticed that James had become intensely lonely. His marriage had been a good one and he longed for another woman who could provide the same joy. It was an act of respect for what he shared with Ida, not an abandonment of her memory, that made him open to finding another wife—a relationship he was to never enjoy again.

Not that James Corrigan had been monogamous. He had enjoyed the occasional favors of other women, something his wealth enabled him to do with little risk of discovery. By contrast, his surviving son, Jimmy, a young man who had not been on the *Idler* that day, was a playboy typical of the first generation of male society leaders who made a career out of inheriting. Jimmy was regularly defending himself privately and, at least once, in court because of his determination to seduce every woman who appealed to him, no matter what he might have to say to get her to bed. The most famous of his indiscretions, and proof of the anti-female attitude of the day, came when Georgiana Young sued him for breach of promise after an affair during his undergraduate years at Cleveland's Case School of Applied Sciences (now Case-Western Reserve University). She sought $50,000, an enormous sum, yet a token of the Corrigan family's worth, and her victory seemed certain when Jimmy's attorney admitted that his client had made all manner of promises to get the woman into bed.

In a defense that seems shocking today, the attorney convinced the jury that any normal, healthy bachelor Jimmy's age and with his financial means would sow wild oats before settling down. Lying to the girl about his future intentions was a common technique for achieving such ends, and a sensible girl would have known that. She made her choice, and even if she came to regret it, there was no reason she should receive such a large sum of money.

The combination of the loss of his family and the reprehensible behavior of his only surviving child led Captain Corrigan to briefly flee the city, traveling with his brother and even more traumatized sister-in-law to the White Sulphur Springs resort in French Lick, Indiana. It was there that Captain James Corrigan was said to have met Laura McMartin, who was also vacationing.

Another story about the Corrigan/McMartin meeting involves a third-party introduction after Laura met and charmed James's sister-in-law. Supposedly, the sister-in-law invited the doctor's wife to the Cleveland estate where she would be able to meet the emotionally shattered Corrigan.

No matter how it happened, Cleveland's society leaders were certain that Laura was an opportunist. They noted that she was a married woman who was visiting a rich widower. It was assumed that as a laborer's daughter turned doctor's wife she was already in a higher-status relationship than she deserved. How dare she go after the wealthy Clevelander?

Laura McMartin's pedigree may not have matched their own, but when it came to intelligence, she was knowledgeable about the affairs of the day, witty, attractive and charming. She had the personality expected of someone who was not only married to a successful man but could also understand and thus share in his professional life.

Perhaps the most important fact of all about the relationship is that Laura McMartin never seduced nor was seduced by James Corrigan. She became a friend and a frequent guest at the Corrigan estate, but they were not lovers. There was no effort to find a way to obtain some of Corrigan's money. Over the period of several years that they were friends, nothing untoward ever happened.

The problem for the female leaders of Cleveland society was that Laura seemed to have more access to the elder Corrigan's estate than they did. And, of course, there was that little matter of Laura McMartin never having been "one of us."

JIMMY CORRIGAN

Laura McMartin knew about her friend James's son, Jimmy. She knew that James held the young man in disdain both for what happened in college and for his postgraduate "career" devoted to womanizing. She never met the young man, though, for she was more welcome on the estate than he was. What she did learn was that Jimmy had drifted west, taking jobs ranging from mining to bartending, the last profession practiced in San Francisco.

It was fortunate that Price McKinney, Corrigan's longtime friend and business partner, had more compassionate understanding of the father/son dynamics than did the captain. James tried to arrange to leave his estate to Price's children instead of his surviving son. Price, believing the action was wrong, located Jimmy and arranged for him to return to Cleveland to meet with his father, hopefully with the males reconciling their differences.

The meeting was as satisfactory as it could be. Jimmy would be the sole heir to his father's estate, but he would not be given direct access to it until he was forty, and even then it wasn't certain. The distribution of the money in the years to come would be handled by James's trusted friends Price McKinney and James E. Ferris. Then, at age forty, Jimmy's actions and lifestyle would be evaluated by McKinney and Ferris. If they approved, the great wealth would pass into Jimmy's total control.

The timing of the financial arrangement was fortuitous. James was just fifty-nine years of age and staying in his Cleveland town house at 8114 Euclid Avenue when he developed extreme pain in his right side. Before he could be helped, he died from appendicitis. The year was 1908, and both Jimmy and Laura came to the funeral, where they met for the first time.

Once more, stories would come to be told about the facts of what took place that year. Supposedly, Jimmy was smitten with Laura, and Laura was smitten with Jimmy's inheritance, despite the fact that she was still married to the doctor and would remain so for another eight apparently monogamous years. However, the same reasons that Dr. McMartin was relegated to working in hotels led to Laura's inability to continue with her marriage. She was divorced in 1916.

How Laura handled the time between her divorce and the next meeting with Jimmy when he realized that, for the first time in his life, he was in love with a woman he wanted to marry, apparently involved again working for the hotel. Years later, society columnist Elsa Maxwell allegedly (and rather snidely) filled in the blanks when she wrote in her book, *Art of the Hostess*:

> *A great London Hostess in the twenties was the irrepressible Laura Corrigan, who established a formidable handicap in the American Cinderella Derby by covering the ground from switchboard operator to rich widow in a record six months.*

If accurate, Laura apparently walked away from her marriage without receiving money from the doctor.

Friends of James Corrigan, who had enjoyed Laura's presence on the Corrigan estate while James was alive, looked at her differently when, eight years after his death, she and Jimmy planned to marry. There was the money, of course. There was the fact that Laura was seven years older than Jimmy in an era when a May/December romance was supposed to involve a younger woman and older man, not the other way around. But the greatest problem remained that to Cleveland society, Laura simply wasn't one of them.

Price McKinney and his wife did not know what to make of what was happening, especially when, after marrying Laura, Jimmy bought a $15,000 lavender Rolls-Royce (more than a quarter of a million dollars in today's money) and had his new bride driven to the estate accompanied by a liveried footman and the former chauffeur for railroad magnate and gold speculator Jay Gould. The latter had little to do with Cleveland, but the name-dropping ensured that the entrance gained public attention.

As Elsa Maxwell noted, the marriage between Laura and Jimmy was short-lived. On January 24, 1928, Jimmy was standing in front of the Cleveland Athletic Club on Euclid Avenue when he suffered a heart attack. He was taken into the lobby so emergency care could be administered, but it was too late. He was dead. It was what happened during the almost ten years—not six months—between marriage and untimely widowhood that added to the Laura Corrigan legend.

Immediately after her marriage to Jimmy, Laura attempted to become a part of Cleveland society. She had a massive estate to use for entertaining, and because such entertaining was expected of the super rich, Laura attempted to involve herself in society activities that had previously been the sole domain of those whose position was earned through inheritance, not marriage. Laura and her efforts at entertaining were generally snubbed.

Deeply hurt, Laura and Jimmy decided that they needed to relocate, choosing Manhattan as the ideal place to live.

New York proved a mixed blessing. Enough of New York's wealthy society leaders were first-generation money so they were less snobbish about Laura's lack of pedigree. It did not take long for her to become friends with the Astors and with Mrs. William Randolph Hearst, the wife of the media mogul who openly spent his life in San Simeon with Marion Davies, his longtime mistress.

Unfortunately for Laura and Jimmy, there was more disdain than welcoming. The elite families of the era were interconnected through business, marriage and schools. One could not talk about New York society without also talking about Cleveland, Philadelphia, Boston, Chicago, Detroit and the like. Some of New York's elite accepted the couple for who and what they were. Others shunned them on general principles because their friends and relatives explained that the Corrigan couple's past was worthy of disdain.

Finally recognizing that she and her husband were rich beyond avarice and that money alone should make them acceptable in society—a reality of the day—Laura Corrigan turned her back on the entire East Coast/ Midwest social scene. She and Jimmy boarded a boat and departed for Europe, arriving in 1921.

EUROPE

The story of those early years in Europe had little to do with Cleveland. The couple began renting and buying homes in every city where they enjoyed living. Jimmy maintained a suite in Cleveland's Statler Hotel from which he could be close to his business interests when he returned to Ohio. Laura arranged for the couple to buy a mansion in Palm Beach, a villa near Rome, an apartment in the Paris Ritz and other properties. She also felt that it was time for Jimmy to be treated like an adult, a professional who understood the business that was the primary source of the couple's money.

Laura Corrigan, the woman society leaders wanted to believe was lacking in intelligence because of her blue-collar breeding, found ways for Jimmy to take full control of Corrigan-McKinney Steel. No longer would he be under the scrutiny of Price McKinney, and no longer would his business actions have to be second-guessed.

The takeover was completed in 1925, an action that shocked Price McKinney. Perhaps he was upset that he could no longer fulfill his late friend's desire to ensure that the wealth would not be squandered. Perhaps he was upset that the company he and James had built from nothing was no longer one in which he had influence. Perhaps he was depressed from the awareness that so many of his friends were dead and he was getting older. Whatever the case, on April 13, 1926, two years before Jimmy's untimely death, Price McKinney took his own life. Approximately nine years later and almost seven years after Jimmy's death, Laura Corrigan returned to Cleveland to sell her stock in Corrigan-McKinney in order to facilitate the creation of Republic Steel. In exchange, in addition to all she owned from her marriage to Jimmy and inheritance at the time of his death, she received a tax-free lifetime annual payment of $800,000.

It was Elsa Maxwell who provides the best look at Laura in the years when she was working to be a part of European society:

> *She was not beautiful, she was not educated or particularly clever—her innocent blunders of speech provided almost as much amusement, behind her back, as her parties—but she was honest, she had vitality, and she had a heart as big as her bank. Laura ran her parties like a particularly benevolent mistress of ceremonies on a well-backed giveaway show. Guests were showered with favors, and as her taste in these ran to gold and precious stones, practical-minded hypocrites found it easy to swallow their prejudices against Laura's lowly beginnings on the grounds that being her guest was the next best thing to being gainfully employed. Laura had good friends who liked her for herself, but there were many more, I'm afraid, who toadied to her for what they could get out of it.*
>
> *Yet for all her love of money show, Laura was not a money snob. She never forgot that she'd come by her millions more or less by default, and that others were not as rich as she. She went out of her ways to see that guests were not obliged to dip into their own pockets for the least thing—even such incidentals as tipping: "The staff is paid extra when guests are staying*

Laura Corrigan

Laura Corrigan. *Courtesy of Cleveland State University's Cleveland Press Collection.*

with me," read signs posted in each of her guestrooms, *"so they do not expect anything from you. Neither do I wish you to give it."*

Maxwell explained that Laura's one snobbery was no different from what would be seen in other wealthy Americans abroad, such as the Kennedy family of Boston. She delighted in having the company of royalty and frequently had them as guests to her parties, a situation that had at least one humorous story, according to Maxwell:

> *There was the time she planned a dinner party in honor of the late Prince George, Duke of Kent. All the invitations were out, when, on the day before the party, the Duke thought better of the idea and sent his regrets. Laura went to work, putting pressure on everyone she knew to provide a suitable royal substitute to fill the place of honor. She managed finally to commandeer King Alphonso of Spain and with this slight change in cast, the party went off as scheduled. The hostess's explanation to her other guest? "Where a Prince refused," said Laura dryly, "a King obliged."*

The royal relationships went beyond a single incident. Laura became close friends with King George VI and Queen Elizabeth. She also recognized that she was making few visits back to Cleveland and that she stayed at the Wade Park Manor when she did. Nagirroc might have been beautiful, but it was no longer needed. Laura put it up for sale.

Laura also had what may have been the most watched transfer of funds ever experienced in Cleveland in April 1938. The Corrigan money had been maintained in the Union Trust Company at Chester Avenue and East Ninth Street. Laura wanted to change to National City Bank. This meant loading what eventually came to be three Brinks armored trucks that would transport the money to the Vincent Avenue (Short Vincent) entrance. The move, approximately a block in length, involved twenty armed guards lining the street, ready to shoot. In addition, police officers and plainclothes officers were seemingly everywhere. The reason was that the trucks carried an estimated $21 million. In addition, two bank officers hand carried suitcases, one of which had $3 million in bonds and the other had $8 million in government securities.

All of the notoriety added to the image of Laura Corrigan as a social climber, royalty lover and money hungry widow who married her way to fortune. What went unsaid was her compassion for others.

World War II had started, and the Nazis were occupying parts of France. Laura had long loved Paris and refused to allow a city about which she was passionate suffer in ways she could alleviate.

Laura first tried to spend her money to help the soldiers and refugees facing the Nazis, but the American government froze her assets. They did not want her great wealth leaving the United States, especially with her living in an area partially under Hitler's control.

There was no stopping Laura. The world that had brought her so much pleasure was going through its own type of hell. She applied to the Nazis to be allowed to travel from Vichy to Paris, and to the surprise of many, she was given permission to travel. She brought along as many items of value as she could carry with her and, once in Paris, negotiated the sale of her jewels to a German syndicate. Then she took all the money and began spending it to help the refugees and others victimized by the war.

Laura's actions were endearing as much as they were critical to the survival of many. For example, unused to living as a normal Parisian, Laura at first turned to the same location to buy food—sandwiches in this instance—as she had done when having personal guests. Instead of going to local bakeries that were still in operation, places with which she had had no personal experience before the war, she went where she knew the staff: the Ritz Hotel. And until she learned less expensive ways to help more people, the men and women in bread lines were suddenly eating food of a quality they could not afford to enjoy when the world was still stable.

Gradually, Laura sold everything of value she owned, including most of her clothing. She retained two dresses, her two wedding rings, her wristwatch and a string of pearls, the latter her one affectation, as they were worth $350,000. Then, with France having fallen to the Nazis, she relocated to Vichy to work with refugees. She lived in a building where six women, in addition to Laura, all shared the same bathroom.

The wartime activities of Laura Corrigan were little known in Cleveland as they were taking place. She pursued the relief effort with the same ardor with which she had once pursued the perfect dinner party. The men and women needing help came from backgrounds not much different from the one in which she had been raised. She knew what it was to survive through laboring and then to lose even that. She had never known hunger, but she had known what it was like to be uncertain where she would live or what she would be able to do to put food on the table. And from her upbringing and the people displaced by the Nazis, she developed compassion previously unseen from Americans living in war-torn France.

It was January 1948 when Laura Corrigan returned to the United States. Her money had been freed, and she was both continuing relief efforts and returning to entertaining in London and Paris. The 1948 trip was to New York, where she planned to visit a sister who had been living in San Francisco while Laura was abroad. In yet another bit of irony in her life, she became ill and died on January 22, exactly twenty years to the day after the death of Jimmy Corrigan.

Society leaders in Cleveland were certain that there would be local benefits from Laura's estate. After all, this was where she had befriended James Corrigan. This was where she had married Jimmy Corrigan. This was where…well, no one wanted to think of the snubs, the backbiting, the sheer bitchiness of the treatment she received, first in Cleveland and then, albeit to a lesser degree, in New York.

Laura remembered, though. Apart from the charitable giving, not a single bequest went to anyone from Cleveland or New York. The woman who had been victimized by snobs turned her back on them all, winning at last.

OBITUARY FOR LAURA MAE CORRIGAN

New York Times, *Saturday, January 24, 1948*

Mrs. Laura Mae Corrigan, widow of James W. Corrigan, Cleveland steel company head, died on Thursday at Post Graduate Hospital here. Mrs. Corrigan was one of England's best known social leaders during the period after the First World War and in the recent war had won many decorations for her work in behalf of soldiers and refugees. She arrived in this country from Paris on Christmas Eve to visit her sister, Mrs. David Armstrong-Taylor of San Francisco. The two sisters had been staying at the Plaza Hotel since then. Mrs. Corrigan became ill on Wednesday and was taken to the hospital.

FABULOUS SOCIETY STORY—The story of Laura Mae Corrigan was a fabulous one in the annals of international society. She was born in Wisconsin. Her father was said to have been an "odd jobs" man and she, herself, to have once been a waitress in Chicago. These stories, despite the lack of any stigma pertaining to them, caused her exclusion from Cleveland society after her marriage to Mr. Corrigan, who was president of the Corrigan-McKinney Steel Company and a son of the founder of the business.

Snubbed on Euclid Avenue, the Corrigans came to New York, but met the same treatment here. According to the society writers of the period immediately after the First World War, Mrs. Corrigan vainly spent "hundreds of thousands" of dollars in attempts to get into Gotham's social swim. Shortly after the war she and her husband went to London, where in the course of time she met Mrs. George Keppel, famous as having been King Edward VII's favorite hostess. Mrs. Corrigan rented Mrs. Keppel's mansion on Grosvenor Street, which had been the scene of many a lavish party for the haute monde. She learned the secrets of success in entertaining royalty and was reputed to have hired Mrs. Keppel's coterie of butlers, footmen and other servants, whose drawing room manners were unmatched anywhere in the world.

MECCA FOR PRINCES, DUKES—Soon the Corrigan mansion was the Mecca of princes, ambassadors and dukes. By 1923, Mrs. Corrigan was virtually London's prime social arbiter. The only element lacking, strangely enough, was "the Knickerbocker crowd." No Astors, Vanderbilts or others bearing old New York—or Cleveland—names were ever invited. The climax came when the phenomenally wealthy prince of India turned down a previous invitation to attend a party at the home of a leading American family of the "Knickerbocker" set in order to accept one at Mrs. Corrigan's. When the Corrigans returned here, society columnists tried to make up to them by declaring in print that they "had not been deserted" by their friends here and had really just gone abroad to amuse themselves. But the breach with Cleveland society was never patched up. Euclid Avenue had become afraid of the Corrigans and Mrs. Corrigan no longer cared. Mr. Corrigan died on Jan. 22, 1928, exactly twenty years before his wife. He was then 47 years old. Later Mrs. Corrigan went abroad again and once more shone in London society, although she had a clash with the Mountbattens and once committed the error of showing the door to an uninvited guest, who, she afterwards discovered was a member of the British royal household.

ORGANIZED "LA BIENVENUE"—Before the outbreak of the recent war, she went to France and immediately upon the commencement of hostilities organized a group of French and other Allied women into "La Bienvenue," a group dedicated to supplying comforts for the soldiers. Her outstanding work in this respect led her to be later decorated with the "Croix du Combatant" by the French Government—one of the very few women ever so decorated because the award is only given for work in the front lines. After the Nazi victory of 1940 she went to Unoccupied France, where she specialized in work for refugees. She was afterwards decorated with the Croix de Guerre and made a member of the Legion of Honor for this work, in pursuit of which she liquidated much of her personal fortune, including her jewelry. Eventually escaping through Portugal, she turned up in London in 1944, where she organized the "Wings Club," which became famous as a haven for Allied aviators. It was established in the former mansion of Lord Moyne, and the Duchess of Kent was chief patroness. The King's Medal was bestowed upon her by Britain for her work. Besides her sister, Mrs. Corrigan leaves a nephew, Duncan Armstrong-Taylor.

About the Author

As the *Cleveland Plain Dealer* put it in April 2009, "Ted Schwarz may be the most prolific author you've never heard of." He's been freelancing full time for nearly forty years. During that time, he's written well over one hundred books and more than three thousand articles and short stories for publications throughout the world. His books have been translated into more than a half dozen languages, and several have been made into documentaries and/or television movies. He has appeared on over three hundred television and radio programs in the United States and Canada, ranging from *Larry King Live* to Dee Perry's *Around Noon* for Cleveland's WCPN, the local NPR station.

Visit us at
www.historypress.net